METAL
CLAY BEADS

METAL CLAY BEADS

TECHNIQUES • PROJECTS • INSPIRATION

Barbara Becker Simon

LARK BOOKS

A Division of
Sterling Publishing Co., Inc.
New York / London

Senior Editor
Marthe Le Van

Production Editor
Nathalie Mornu

Art Directors
Thom Gaines
Robin Gregory

Photo Stylist
Dana Irwin

Project Photography
Stewart O'Shields

How-To Photography
Rob Stegmann

Illustrator
Orrin Lundgren

Cover Designer
Robin Gregory

COVER
BARBARA BECKER SIMON
Red Rocks, 2005
Largest bead, 5 x 3 x 1.5 cm
Fine silver, stainless steel,
granite, basalt, sterling silver;
hollow box beads
PHOTO BY LARRY SANDERS

PAGE 2
BARBARA BECKER SIMON
Peaches in Regalia, 2000

Library of Congress Cataloging-in-Publication Data

Simon, Barbara Becker.
  Metal clay beads : techniques, projects, inspiration / Barbara Becker Simon. -- 1st ed.
     p. cm.
  Includes index.
  ISBN 978-1-60059-025-2 (HC-PLC with jacket : alk. paper)
  1. Jewelry making. 2. Precious metal clay. 3. Beads. I. Title.
  TT212.S552 2009
  745.58'2--dc22

                                              2008042308

10 9 8 7 6 5 4 3 2 1

First Edition

Published by Lark Books, A Division of
Sterling Publishing Co., Inc.
387 Park Avenue South, New York, NY 10016

© 2009, Barbara Becker Simon
Photography © 2009, Lark Books unless otherwise specified
Illustrations © 2009, Lark Books unless otherwise specified
Photo of faceted stone on page 37 © Jupiterimages Corporation

Distributed in Canada by Sterling Publishing,
c/o Canadian Manda Group, 165 Dufferin Street
Toronto, Ontario, Canada M6K 3H6

Distributed in the United Kingdom by GMC Distribution Services,
Castle Place, 166 High Street, Lewes, East Sussex, England BN7 1XU

Distributed in Australia by Capricorn Link (Australia) Pty Ltd.,
P.O. Box 704, Windsor, NSW 2756 Australia

The written instructions, photographs, designs, patterns, and projects in this volume
are intended for the personal use of the reader and may be reproduced for that purpose
only. Any other use, especially commercial use, is forbidden under law without written
permission of the copyright holder.

Every effort has been made to ensure that all the information in this book is accurate.
However, due to differing conditions, tools, and individual skills, the publisher cannot
be responsible for any injuries, losses, and other damages that may result from the use
of the information in this book.

If you have questions or comments about this book, please contact:
Lark Books
67 Broadway
Asheville, NC 28801
828-253-0467

Manufactured in China

ISBN 13: 978-1-60059-025-2

For information about custom editions, special sales, and premium and corporate
purchases, please contact Sterling Special Sales Department at 800-805-5489 or
specialsales@sterlingpub.com.

BARBARA BECKER SIMON
Glass/PMC Bead Group, 2006
Largest, 3.3 x 1.5 x 1.5 cm
Glass, fine-silver spools; lampworked
PHOTO BY ROBERT DIAMANTE

CONTENTS

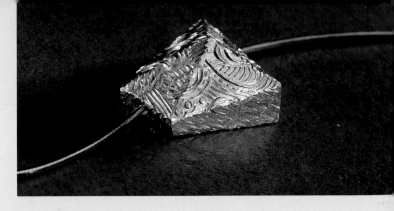

As I leafed through my issue of a national jewelry magazine in the fall of 1995, the pages opened to an article written by Tim McCreight about a material that behaved like clay and consisted of microscopic particles of pure, precious metal. As I read on, my jaw dropped open and my brain began to race, calculating the possibilities this stuff could achieve.

For 25 years before this upheaval, I had pursued a career making one-of-a-kind jewelry. I was no stranger to high-karat gold, diamonds, and emeralds, and all the techniques that combine these items. I hammered, I sawed, I filed, I soldered, and I cast. I also taught on the college level and was well versed in conveying information on all manner of metalworking procedures. But this metal clay was something new, revolutionary, and impossibly magical!

Metal clay wasn't yet being marketed in the United States. I was like a Knight of the Round Table on a quest to get my hands on the Holy Grail of this miraculous clay. In my search, I wrote letters and made calls and seven months later finally purchased six ounces.

Those lumps of clay sat in a drawer out of sight for months. They called to me, but I was petrified I'd fail to make something fabulous and worthy from this precious material. (There was also the minor detail that I had no idea how to manipulate, fire, or finish the metal clay.)

INTRODUCTION

BARBARA BECKER SIMON
Ant Bead, 1999
4 x 4 cm
Fine silver; hollow bead created on complex core
PHOTO BY ROBERT DIAMANTE

Destiny answered and a wonderful organization to which I belong, the Florida Society of Goldsmiths, held a weeklong metal clay workshop in January, 1997—taught by none other than Tim McCreight. In class that first morning, when I opened my packet of clay and began making my first piece, I knew it would completely change my approach to jewelry making.

Metal clay has expanded my aesthetic and technical vocabularies, but most of all, it has given me the privilege to teach and pass on new and important knowledge for the pleasure of my fellow jewelry makers, while allowing me to make new and fast friends and travel the world.

In this book, I intend to emphasize what is, to me, metal clay's most important advantage in the realm of jewelry making: creating hollow forms. As a formally trained metalworker and jeweler, I know what it takes to create beads using traditional methods. The procedures can be rewarding and the results spectacular. However, employing lost wax casting or construction techniques

BARBARA BECKER SIMON
Metal Clay Bead Group, 2003
Largest, 3 x 1.5 x 3 cm
Fine silver; complex core, box construction
PHOTO BY LARRY SANDERS

to create a bead involves extensive education, considerable financial outlay for tools, and time to perfect the processes.

Using metal clay to form a bead involves much less time, tools, and technology. In addition, I dare say metal clay can accomplish some techniques that would tax the skills of a master jeweler. The accessibility and user-friendly characteristics of metal clay allow anyone to successfully create beautiful beads.

The first part of this book concerns itself with the material and how to use it. I've included chapters that relate to embellishment and texturing. The remainder of the book consists of 22 bead projects of varying degrees of difficulty. I've tried to include every method I know to create a hollow form. Try these projects, and then take the principles of making metal clay beads to have fun creating some new forms of your own.

BARBARA BECKER SIMON
Pinctada Maximus, 2003
50 cm long
Fine silver, fine gold, sterling silver,
South Sea pearls, glass; bimetal
hollow box beads
PHOTO BY LARRY SANDERS

THE
BASICS

WHAT IS METAL CLAY?

Dr. M. Morikawa
COURTESY OF
MITSUBISHI MATERIALS
CORPORATION

Metalwork and jewelry are disciplines with traditions thousands of years old. Casting has been a jewelry-making procedure for 3,000 years. Stamping and die cutting have been used in the metals industry for more than a century. Today, new techniques and materials are few and far between. About 10 years ago, a Japanese scientist, Dr. M. Morikawa, invented metal clay, giving the jewelry community a material that allows everyone, including those with no metal-working experience, to make astounding precious-metal objects.

Metal clay consists of three ingredients: finely powdered pure metal, organic binder, and water. The metal is usually a precious or noble metal—one that won't form an oxide layer when heated. Silver, gold, and gold-silver mixtures are the typical components. Recent developments have allowed the introduction of base metal materials to the metal clay world. The first is bronze clay, and others such as copper clay may follow. The binder is a type of food additive that, along with the other ingredients, makes metal clay completely safe and nontoxic. In correct proportion, the metal, binder, and water result in a smooth, claylike substance that easily allows the user to employ myriad techniques to achieve texture and shape.

Metal clay is available in a number of different forms and formulas. The most commonly used comes in lump form. You can shape clay in this state into almost any profile. Slip and looser syringe clay result when more binder and water are added. Slip can serve as a decorative material, a form of "glue," or a means of building up a form. Metal clay also exists in sheets known as metal clay paper. Syringe and paper can save lots of time in realizing certain decorative surfaces.

Metal clay, depending on the size and shape of the microscopic particles of metal and the proportion of binder and water, has a couple of distinctive properties, specifically firing time and temperature. The first type of metal clay that was—and still is—available fired at 1650°F (898.9°C) for 2 hours with no variation in time or temperature. This clay has a shrinkage rate of about 28 percent. Next are the medium-firing clays that require much lower temperatures (1425–1560°F [773.9–848.9°C]) and shorter firing times. The medium clays shrink about 12 percent. Last on the scene are the metal clays that can be fired between 1110 and 1290°F (598.9 and 698.9°C) for as little as 10 minutes. These have a shrinkage rate between 8 and 12 percent.

The firing schedule for bronze clay differs from those of the noble metal clays. With the clay piece in it, ramp the kiln up slowly, 250°F (121.1°C) per hour, to 1525°F (829.4°C). This ramping stage will take about 6 hours. Hold the kiln at 1550°F (843.3°C) for 3 hours, for a total firing time of 9 hours. Bronze metal clay shrinks about 5 percent after drying, and an additional 7 to 12 percent after firing. The range of shrinkage depends on the size and shape of the item.

No matter which brand or type of metal clay you choose to work with, follow the manufacturer's recommended firing schedule.

TIM MCCREIGHT
Untitled, 2006
Diameter, 2.2 cm
Fine silver, 22-karat gold; overlay
PHOTO BY ROBERT DIAMANTE

Basic Tool Kit

Every project calls for a Basic Tool Kit. I list its contents below. Other tools will be added to the Basic Tool Kit as the project requires.

- Main work surface
- Small pieces of acetate, overhead projector film, or Teflon
- Rolling pin
- Olive oil or other lubricant/release agentt
- Needle tool
- Craft knife or razor blade
- Paintbrushes
- Caulking tool/spatula tool
- Abrasives: emery files, sheet of 180- or 200-grit emery paper, foam pads, steel wool, etc.
- Spacers
- Water and container
- Drill bits in various sizes
- Ruler
- Sharp pencil
- Paper
- Scissors
- Drinking straw
- Coffee stirrer/beverage straw
- Plastic wrap
- Rubber-tipped tool
- Cone-shaped tool
- Vermiculite or fiber blanket

TOOLS AND EQUIPMENT

Your metal clay tool kit will contain many commonplace items such as drinking straws and sponges rather than a lot of jewelry and metal-working tools. Do note that it's important not to mix noble metal clays and bronze clay in the unfired state; I recommend a separate set of tools for working with bronze clay (see page 18).

A Work Surface

It's never a good idea to build your metal clay pieces directly on a table surface because the clay may stick or pick up the texture of the table. You need a waterproof work surface free of texture of any kind. Many people rest a sheet of plastic or glass on top of their worktable. Use a size similar to a piece of paper, about 8 x 12 inches (20.3 x 30.5 cm). Kitchen supply departments usually have smooth plastic or non-textured glass cutting boards that work just fine.

In addition, I like to place a quarter sheet of overhead projector film or acetate over the work surface. This allows me to pick up the work-in-progress and turn it around or transfer it easily to another place without having to lift anything else.

Tools for Making Sheets

One of the main forms we use for construction of metal beads is the sheet. Use these tools for making sheets.

Rolling Pin. Although you can buy commercial rolling pins specifically designed for metal clay, the tool I prefer for rolling it out is a piece of thick-walled PVC pipe about ¾ inch (1.9 cm) in diameter and 8 or 9 inches (20.3 or 22.9 cm) long. Most hardware or home improvement stores will cut a piece of pipe to that length. You can also cut it with a hacksaw.

Spacers. Scraps of mat board, craft sticks, and plastic strips are useful for making sheets of metal clay of uniform thickness. Place them on either side of the lump of clay you're about to roll out into a broad, flat piece.

I like to use plastic-coated playing cards as spacers. In fact, because they're easy to stack to various thicknesses, they've become the standard unit of the metal clay world. Directions for construction often state that a certain component should be three cards thick or five cards thick. This refers to the number of playing cards stacked on either side of the clay. A time-saving device is to glue together cards to create sets of permanent spacers. For instance, glue seven cards together with a number 7 card of any suit on top, and you'll always know it's a seven-spacer.

Lubricants and Release Agents

Metal clay can adhere in an undesirable way to surfaces and materials. Release agents and lubricants help prevent this "sticky" situation.

Olive Oil. A few drops of olive oil prevent metal clay from sticking to your hands or other surfaces. I also find solid lip and body balms with olive oil as the main ingredient very convenient. They don't spill as easily, and they smell good, too!

Coat all brand-new tools with a delicate film of olive oil. Over time, all your metal clay tools will become permeated with oil and you'll no longer have to grease them. Too much lubricant will cause your tools to slip and slide on the clay, however, so be stingy with the amount applied.

Powder Pouncer. I cut a 6-inch (15.2 cm) square from an old T-shirt, put about 1 tablespoon (15 grams) of talcum powder in the center, and gather up the ends and secure them snugly with a rubber band. This powder dispenser deposits a fine layer of talcum on any surface you don't want your clay to stick to. I use this on some of the texture sheets for ease of clay removal.

Tools for Keeping Clay Moist

For perfect working conditions, your metal clay should retain the degree of moisture it has when you first open the packet. These tools will help maintain that workability.

Water and Containers. When I work, I use several different methods for moisturizing my clay. Sometimes you need a lot of water and other times only a bit. I always have a small cup or bowl of water nearby. Another small, low container holds a piece of cellulose sponge and a quantity of water that reaches halfway up the side of the sponge. This allows me to dip my brush into a very small amount of liquid rather than completely submerging my brush and getting a lot of water.

Another source of water is a small spray bottle. I don't use it often, but when a surface needs an overall fine misting, this is the way to do it. You can find small spray bottles at discount stores in the cosmetic section.

Plastic Wrap. Use kitchen plastic wrap to keep metal clay moist by sealing it off from drafts and dry air. If you're working only with a small amount of lump clay, cover the rest of it with a sheet of plastic wrap to keep it from drying out. I wrap leftover lumps of clay in plastic as well before storing them in plastic bags.

Clay "Garages." While working with the clay, it's necessary to keep it covered and yet easily accessible. Because it takes extra work to unwrap and wrap each time I need an additional bit of clay, I use an old plastic yogurt cup that I've modified by securing a piece of damp sponge in the bottom. I then upend the yogurt cup on a teacup saucer. I can "park" a lump of clay under the cup for hours as I work, without it drying out. Other methods and contraptions will serve the same purpose. Do whatever works for you; it pays to keep that clay moist.

Paintbrushes. I have several different kinds of brushes at my work area. First, and probably most important, is a small—about a size 2—pointed round brush, which I use to apply water to clay. There's no need to buy an expensive brush, but don't use cheap ones either, because, annoyingly, the hairs fall out and get on your clay. Constant use on metal clay is hard on this small brush, so you'll need to replace it as it loses its ability for pinpoint action.

Cutting Tools

Not all designs for metal clay beads use pieces of clay torn from the lump; frequently, we need to separate and cut the clay in very precise ways.

Needle Tool. This tool allows you to trace, pierce, mark, and decorate your metal clay. This is easily obtained from ceramic supply houses, or you can make your own by embedding a heavy-gauge sewing needle into a cork or baking it into a polymer clay handle.

Knives. The ability to cut metal clay is essential. My favorite tool for this is a craft knife. I use it to cut wet clay, to score and cut dry clay, and as a scraping tool.

I also have something called a tissue blade in my kit. This is a very thin, sharp blade about 4 inches (10.2 cm) long. Because it's so thin, it slices a very precise line and can even be bent into a slight arc to cut a curve. Tissue blades are available from scientific supply houses and some metal clay tool vendors. As an alternative, long thin blades can often be found in the polymer clay section of craft stores. These aren't as thin as tissue blades, but they do the job as well.

Drill Bits. We often have to drill holes in dry clay, and sometimes in a fired piece. Use steel drill bits of various sizes for this task. With dry clay so easy to pierce, it's not necessary to use mechanical means to power the drill. For ease of use, I mount drill bits in polymer handles and bake them; I also fix them a pin vise for this purpose.

A good selection to have is a #60 (0.04 inch [1 mm]) for really small holes, a #36 (0.11 inch [2.7 mm]) for medium holes, and a #28 (0.14 inch [3.6 mm]) for larger holes. None of these sizes is absolute: whatever you can find in the general size range will work. As you progress, you may find you want more variety in drill bits.

Punches. Craft stores sell decorative punches, usually in the scrapbooking section. I've also used the plain hole punches meant for paper found in office supply stores. Metal clay paper can be die cut with these tools.

Cookie Cutters. I apply this term to the variety of metal tools that cut clay into predetermined shapes, such as circles and leaf forms. You can find them in craft stores, usually in the polymer clay section, or make your own out of thin-gauge brass, using tin snips to cut the metal and pliers to bend it.

Shaping Tools

These items help manipulate, move, and remove metal clay.

Paintbrushes. I've already mentioned the size 2 brush (page 13). Besides water application, it's useful for smoothing areas and moving wet clay.

Another type of brush I use is a larger (about a size 10), fluffier round brush. Its soft bristles will gently brush away metal clay dust from the surface of your piece so you can see the area you're working on. A soft makeup brush will do this job as well.

At my work area I also have a very stiff bristle brush for when I need a little "muscle" to brush away dried metal clay from the surface of tools or gemstones. When I sand or engrave a surface, I sometimes need a little springier brush to rid the piece of powder or chips. For that task, I frequently select a flat-bristle paintbrush about ⅝ inch (1.6 cm) wide. The other stiff brush I have is smaller, to get into more compact areas. It has a flat shape and measures about ¼ inch (6 mm) wide.

I put "old" brushes to work as slip or paste applicators. An old and abused brush rather than a new shapely one is best for this operation.

Rubber Fingertips. Potters and sculptors who work with ceramic clay are the most frequent users of rubber fingertips. This tool has a handle like a paintbrush, but the tip is made of flexible rubber. The tips can be round and pointy, knife-edged, or any number of other shapes. The one I use most has a round, pointed tip about ⅜ inch (1 cm) in diameter by about ½ inch (1.3 cm) long. It's like having a teeny fingertip to smooth and manipulate the clay when your own finger is too big to fit the bill. You'll find this indispensable tool in some art stores, ceramic supply houses, and most metal clay suppliers.

Plastic Palette Knife. This is the best tool for mixing slip or clay. Look in the painting section of your favorite craft or art supply store to find a selection of these inexpensive miniature trowels.

FAR LEFT
Rubber fingertips
LEFT
Palette knives

TOP
JEANETTE LANDENWITCH
Untitled, 2007
46 cm long
Fine silver metal clay, rutile quartz beads, sterling silver spacer beads; engraved
PHOTO BY ARTIST

BOTTOM
TERRY KOVALCIK
White Shell, 2005
12.9 x 1.4 x 2.4 cm
Fine silver clay; hollow formed, carved
PHOTO BY CORRIN JACOBSEN KOVALCIK

Carving Tools. Carving tools come in various forms and styles. My favorites are the #1 linoleum cutter with handle and the 1-mm V-shaped gouge sold by some of the polymer clay suppliers and model maker suppliers. I use them to create decorative patterns on metal clay and to create texture sheets. I've also used very small chisels and traditional metalwork tools called gravers to carve, but more frequently I utilize these for scraping.

Spatula Tools. Out of all my tools, I reach for these the most often; they can fill gaps as well as smooth, scrape, and shape the metal clay. These small spoonlike or spatula-shaped tools are commonly found in jewelry supply catalogs under wax working tools, but I've also found them in sculpture supply stores and at flea markets; some dentists will even give their retired tools to patients.

Armatures and Cores

You can form clay around lightbulbs, plastic Easter eggs, and polymer clay shapes—among other things—to make hollow beads.

Core materials are the substances that you build a form around to create an enclosed hollow object. The perfect core material is easy to obtain, nontoxic, easy to combust with no residue or "hot spots," easy to manipulate, and inexpensive. Many materials have several of these properties. Candidates include compacted paper; balsa wood; papier-mâché; balled-up bread; packing, insulating, and florist foams (expanded styrene); cork clay; wood clay; and various dry food materials, such as snack cheese balls and dog kibble. All these examples work; just determine your preference.

Materials *not* suited for cores are anything wet and organic, such as carrots and potatoes. Paper clay (volcanic ash is listed in the ingredients) isn't suitable for a solid core, although it has its place as a layered

inner support. Cork from a wine bottle isn't a good bet because it expands during firing. A core made of solid wax isn't a good choice either; it gives off toxic fumes when heated to high temperatures. Avoid hardwood as well as the soft wood shapes available at craft stores, which are treated with unknown chemicals that could do harm during the firing process.

As in all matters of incineration, use common sense. I always place my kiln under a ventilation hood when firing an object with a core. If you don't have a ventilation system in your work area, take your kiln outside when firing cored objects.

Abrasives

Abrasives are an essential part of metal clay construction. You'll need certain key tools for abrading or wearing away dry metal clay while dry working. When sanding or filing, the dust is heavy and tends to fall rather than float, but you should consider wearing a dust mask while working if you have any respiratory issues.

Emery Boards. Find these at beauty supply shops in coarse, medium, and fine grits. Use them to clean up ragged edges and bumpy planes, and to otherwise refine shapes that were cut out with more gross tools. Get the biggest ones you can find; later, you can cut them into smaller, more useful shapes using heavy scissors.

Emery Paper. This is the wet-and-dry paper that can be found in the paint departments of home improvement stores and in auto supply stores. Regular sandpaper is *not* the same as wet/dry emery paper and tends to shed little bits of grit as you use it. You don't want to get these stray bits of sand mixed up with your metal clay, so use emery, which doesn't shed.

Useful grits for working with metal clay are 80 to 400; the higher the number, the finer the grit.

Microfinishing Film. You can obtain this high-tech abrasive from jewelry suppliers. Sheets of thin plastic coated with microabrasive offer another, very durable sanding alternative. The grits range from 180 to 4000! They can be cut with scissors into small dimensions, and one form has an adhesive backing that allows you to stick it onto any smooth, flat surface to create a sanding stick.

Micropolishing Paper. These super-fine grit papers can be found in jewelry supply catalogs. The coarsest papers, 400 and 600 grit, can be used for dry work. The finer grits are better for fired clay. **Note:** Emery paper, microfinishing film, and micropo-

lishing paper can all be wrapped around or glued to a backing material, such as craft sticks, wooden beverage stirring sticks, and similar items to give you a custom abrasive tool.

Foam Pads. Abrasive surfaces laminated on a thin foam pad will give you a flexible sander good for convex or concave curved surfaces. You'll find these in the paint sections of home improvement stores or jewelry supply catalogs. They come in grits 80 to 1000 (and as with other abrasives, the smaller the number, the coarser the grit). You can also find a similar tool at beauty supply stores, usually in some sort of block form.

I constantly use small pieces of sponge-backed sanding pads. They range from 80 to 1000 grit and usually come in 4 x 5-inch (10.2 x 12.7 cm) pieces, which I cut into quarters. There are also abrasive sheets, cloths, and films that have finer grits, adhesive backing, and various other attributes. Find what you like to use and stock it in your kit.

Needle Files. These aren't an absolute necessity, but they're really nice for getting into those hard to reach places when doing dry work. Don't buy high-quality files for working with metal clay; instead, get a #2 cut set of twelve 6-inch-long (15.2 cm) files.

Miscellaneous Tools

I like to keep some miscellaneous tools in my kit to perform all kinds of tasks besides the obvious. These include chain-nose pliers, wire nippers, an empty syringe, drinking straws, cocktail straws, toothpicks, craft sticks, straight pins, tape (both masking and cellophane), zip-closure plastic bags in various sizes, a permanent marker, and a pencil. (I particularly like mechanical pencils with 0.5-mm lead because they're always sharp.) A ruler that has both a metric and an inch guide will come in handy for many things. Making paper patterns is often part of hollow construction, and you'll need something to cut them out. You can also use scissors to cut metal clay paper. I have a pair of small, pointy tweezers about 4 inches (10.2 cm) long, which I use to hold and place small items as I work.

Polymer Clay

A package or two of polymer clay will serve many purposes. It's a wonderful design aid, a means of creating texture plates, a mold and armature material, and a vehicle for holding pieces of clay as they dry. When using polymer clay, it's important to keep it and all the tools you use on it separate from the metal clay. After using polymer clay, wipe off all the tools and surfaces and clean up any bits of polymer that could later get mixed into metal clay.

Drying Tools

I often like to speed the drying time of my metal clay, and various ways of aiding this process exist. At the top of my list is my food dehydrator, which naturally isn't used for food anymore. The dehydrator gently blows hot air around the clay. I've placed some plastic needlepoint sheets over the grid of the tray, and I put my metal clay items on it so they won't fall through or pick up much texture.

Other drying tools include electric cup warmers such as those found in drug or department stores, and warming trays for food, which can often be found secondhand in thrift stores. Hair dryers also work for drying clay.

Kilns

A number of companies manufacture kilns specifically designed for metal clay. These are the most convenient to use because they have computer-controlled programs. Whatever kiln you have, you *must* be able to rely on the accuracy of the *pyrometer*—the gauge that records the internal temperature.

There are other means of firing metal clay: ultra-light kilns, butane torches, hot pots, stove tops and the like. Not all these are suitable for some of the projects in this book, but many can be used. Directions and procedures for these items are available from the manufacturer or on the Web.

Finishing Tools and Equipment

After firing, you'll use various materials, tools, and equipment to achieve the desired finish on your metal clay work.

Brass and Stainless Steel Brushes. Stiff metal brushes allow you to impart a satiny finish to the surface of your piece.

Steel Wool. I use 0000 steel wool to impart a soft matte finish.

Powdered Pumice. This fine abrasive also creates a matte finish on fired metal clay.

Burnishers. Use these polished steel tools to rub your fired clay and produce a shiny surface.

Tumblers. Whether it's a rotary tumbler or one of the magnetic machines, this piece of equipment mechanically burnishes fired metal clay to a high shine.

Tools for Bronze Clay

When working with bronze clay, you should have separate work surfaces (including the main surface and Teflon or acetate sheets) and dedicate a set of these tools solely to bronze: rolling pin, paintbrushes, drinking straws, emery boards, and other abrasives. Other tools, such as craft knives, other blades, and needle tools, can be washed before and after working with bronze clay if you don't wish to dedicate them solely to this use.

HATTIE SANDERSON
Untitled, 2007
35 x 12 x 12 cm
Fine silver, glass beads, miscella-
neous beads; lampworked
PHOTO BY ARTIST

FORMING

Forming metal clay really begins with the type of clay you find in the manufacturer's package. Do you have a piece of paper, a syringe, a lump, or a jar of paste? If you have a piece of paper or a syringe, the clay is already in a predetermined shape—a time-saver for you.

The most elemental way to work with metal clay in lump form is to pinch off pieces and begin manipulating the clay with your fingers. This is certainly a viable means of creating a form, and one that needs no further explanation. As you work through the various projects in this book, you'll explore more and more complex refinements in the forming process. But let's start with the basics.

Before you begin, remember that in all forming procedures except for the permanently flexible clay, it's important to keep the clay moist. Pinch off only what you need from a lump and wrap up the rest in a piece of plastic wrap or place it under a plastic cup. Even when working on a project, you might need to cover a component with a sheet of plastic wrap to tend to other things. A judicious amount of water applied with a brush or spray bottle is sometimes needed to maintain the moisture in a piece.

By the way, once a piece of metal clay dries out, it can be reconstituted. Transforming it into very small particles and then gradually adding water will bring the dry material back to clay consistency.

There are two methods for creating a powder of dry metal clay. The first involves breaking the pieces of clay into ½-inch (1.3 cm) pieces and grinding them in a coffee bean grinder until powder is formed. The other is to use a coarse emery sheet, about 180 grit, and file the dry metal clay pieces into a powder.

Making Sheets

Many of the projects in this book need to be made from sheets of metal clay. To create these, you need a clean and texture-free work surface, greased with olive oil, a small piece of acetate, a rolling pin, and a set of spacers that will determine the desired thickness of the sheet. Forming sheets with a consistent thickness is very important for the success of your final product, so practice this technique until your sheets have no thick or thin areas.

1. Rub a drop or two of olive oil on your hands, then preform a lump of metal clay a little by gently compressing it between your palms or fingers into a thick pancake.

2. Place this pancake in the middle of your work surface/acetate and put spacers ½ inch (1.3 cm) to the left and right of the pancake.

3. Place the rolling pin in the center of the pancake, straddling the spacers.

4. Press down with a medium pressure and roll toward you to the end of the clay. You may have to shift the spacers as the clay lengthens. *Don't* roll without spacers: it will result in an inconsistent thickness.

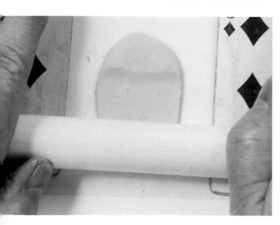

5. Roll back toward the middle with the same pressure. (As you begin rolling in that direction, sometimes the sheet will stick to the rolling pin. Just peel it off and lay it down on the acetate before you continue.) After you reach the center, roll past it to the other end of the clay, shifting the spacers as needed.

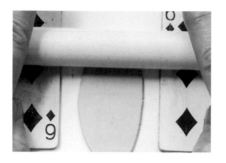

Don't expect to achieve a perfect sheet with one pass. This is the preliminary roll. At this point, gently pick up the sheet and flip it over (doing this prevents the sheet from sticking to the acetate). Next, starting at the edge closest to you and using firm, consistent pressure, roll along the sheet all the way to the farthest edge. Don't forget to shift the spacers as the sheet gets longer. This should give you a smooth sheet of consistent thickness. If it doesn't meet with your approval, just peel it up, flip it, and roll again.

Making Flexible Sheets

If you know your project requires a thin sheet, it's often convenient to use the manufactured paper, which is particularly thin (0.01 inch [0.3 mm] or 30 gauge) and flexible. It's wonderful for folding origami-like structures, draping, weaving, and appliquéing onto other forms of metal clay. It cuts easily with scissors, craft punches, and craft knives.

If you need thicker material than the manufactured sheet, it's possible to make your own flexible sheets. Store these in plastic bags and they'll stay pliant for a long time.

1. Make sure your work surface is lightly oiled. Put about 25 grams of clay on it. Placing a sheet of plastic between the roller and the clay so that less sticking will occur, roll the clay out as thin as possible. (You don't need spacers or cards.)

2. Sprinkle eight drops of glycerin on the surface of the sheet and spread them around with your fingers.

3. Fold the sheet in half and then in half again five or six times until you have a compact lump.

4. Place the lump on your work surface, plastic on top, and roll it thin again. You'll find the clay extremely sticky; use a palette knife to scrape it up into a lump again. Repeat rolling and scraping as many times as needed until the lump feels like regular clay, accomplishing the entire process as speedily as you can so the clay doesn't dry out.

5. Once the clay's consistency has returned to its original state, roll it out to the desired thickness with a plain surface or use a texture plate for a permanent, flexible sheet.

By the way, you can skip step 5 and pack this altered flexible clay into an extruder (see below) to make flexible wire instead. To do this, extrude the wire in long, straight strands. After they dry, they can be coiled in large circles for storage in plastic bags.

Making Worms

Making a round wire form or "worm" of a very small diameter is done very easily by extruding clay from a prepackaged syringe. The extruded clay looks somewhat like piping on a cake and has a diameter of about 0.05 inch (1.3 mm) or 16 gauge.

The package contains an additional plastic tip you can push onto the syringe tip to extrude clay that's about 0.016 inch (0.4 mm) or 26 gauge. If you'd like to end up with a larger diameter, just take a sharp razor blade and trim the plastic point down to the desired size and squirt away!

Some metal clay supply companies also sell custom tips to fit onto the syringe; these extrude square, half-round, curved, and various other profiles.

Using Syringes. Using a syringe is a skill that requires practice. Control with the syringe is based on three things: holding the syringe in your fist with your thumb on the plunger, bracing your hands on one another, and resting your elbows on the table

as you work. In a way, syringe work is like cake decorating, but unlike applying frosting by touching the tip to the surface of the cake, we like our extruded clay to fall through the

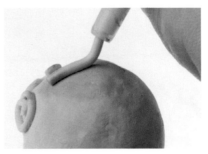

air and then make contact with the surface to be decorated. You achieve better control this way.

Because royal icing matches the consistency of the syringe clay and dries hard, an economical way to gain experience is to mix up a batch of it

Royal Icing

- 2 egg whites
- 2 teaspoons lemon juice
- 3 cups of sifted confectioner's sugar (powdered sugar)

Beat the egg whites and lemon juice together until foamy. Slowly add the sugar, beating until the consistency of the icing is smooth.

(see the box above) or purchase some from a cake-decorating store. You'll need to find an empty syringe in which to pack the icing, then practice with it.

Using Extruders. Another option for making wires are the various clay extruders sold by metal clay suppliers. They have much larger capacities and you must load the clay yourself. Many styles of dies fit into these little machines to allow all kinds of design possibilities. To make up for the drying that takes place as the clay goes through the opening, I always advise people to blend a little extra water into the clay before loading it into these extruding guns.

Hand Rolling. Remember creating "worms" and "snakes" in grade school by rolling a lump of clay back and forth between your palm and the tabletop? With metal clay, we use the same technique. This usually results in an irregular or inconsistent diameter, which may suit you. To make a very even worm, however, roll the clay with a piece of plastic instead of your palm. You can use stiff plastic cut to about 3 x 5 inches (7.6 x 12.7 cm), or a flexible sheet. As you roll it back and forth, the clay tends to dry out, and dry "worms" will crack as you form them for

decorative purposes; one advantage to using a plastic sheet is it helps the clay remain moist. I also like to add a little bit of water to any clay I plan to transform into a worm; that way, it will retain enough flexibility when I'm ready to bend and form it into its final shape. If I get cracks, they're usually minor and easily repaired when the piece is dry.

TOP

BARBARA BECKER SIMON
Box Bead, 2008
1.9 x 1.9 x 0.6 cm
Bronze clay; fired
PHOTO BY ROB STEGMANN

CENTER

YVONNE M. PADILLA
Lava Rock, 2008
2.4 x 3.1 x 0.8 cm
Bronze clay, molded lava rock, patina; fired
PHOTO BY TARA ANDERSON

BOTTOM

YVONNE M. PADILLA
Untitled, 2008
2.5 x 1 cm
Bronze clay, patina; textured, kiln-fired, polished
PHOTO BY TARA ANDERSON

FAR RIGHT

MARGARITE PARKER GUGGOLZ
Nobody Home, 2007
43.5 cm long
Fine silver, 22-karat gold, embroidery cord,
sterling silver, liver of sulfur; formed, fired,
hand fabricated, patinated
PHOTO BY RALPH GABRINER

RIGHT

BARBARA BECKER SIMON
Collage I (detail), 2006
2.5 x 127 cm
Fine silver, glass, granite,
porphyry, stainless steel, sterling
silver, hollow metal clay bead;
lampworked
PHOTO BY LARRY SANDERS

JOINING

Two things are important in joining pieces of metal clay: the strength and integrity of the seam, and the aesthetics—how it looks.

A good seam is one that has a maximum amount of surface area onto which to apply the slip. For instance, in joining a band ring, we would want a lap seam rather than a butt seam because the lap seam has more space for slip and will therefore make a stronger joint.

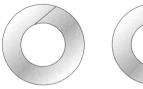

Lap seam   Butt seam

Constructed pieces of metal clay need to be stuck together, and our glue is called *slip*. Slip is primarily used to glue pieces of unfired clay together. Metal clay manufacturers market a thick, creamy product called *paste*, which serves the same purpose. The terms *slip* and *paste* really can be used interchangeably because they perform the same tasks. However, you might find it more economical to mix your own slip and store it in an airtight container. Just be sure to label the container with the specific kind of metal clay slip it contains. **Note:** Only mix as much bronze clay slip as you need for a joint as it oxidizes and becomes useless.

Making Slip

Metal clay can be altered by adding more water for a creamier, runnier consistency. Slip is a ceramics term that describes clay in this condition. You can make your own slip by adding water, drop by drop, to a bit of lump clay, smearing and blending the water in little by little with a plastic palette knife until you arrive at the desired consistency.

The amount of water added to slip is an individual choice, but I like to make my slip about the consistency of thin yogurt. If you need slip of a different viscosity, you can always add more water. The water in slip helps penetrate the sides of the seam being joined so that the connection is successful.

In addition to the glue function, slip/paste can be used as a decorative treatment on the surface of a metal clay piece. Spackling it on in a painterly manner can make for a very interesting texture. This diluted clay can also be painted in multiple layers on convex forms to create hollow objects. You must use eight to 10 layers to achieve a structurally strong object.

Basic Seaming

Paying close attention to the neatness of a seam is a key element in the overall look of a metal clay piece. Unfinished seams call attention to themselves and detract from the success of the piece. Good crafts-manship should always be your goal.

Really fresh, wet clay pieces can simply be joined with a bit of water. However, most often I apply an ample amount of slip to one side of the joint and gently press the two parts together, being careful not to distort any texture or form in the wet clay. It's always a good idea to put a generous application of slip on a seam rather than too little. It doesn't usually matter if the slip oozes out because you can clean up any excess. When joining pieces of metal clay paper, however, be aware that too much moisture will cause the paper to disintegrate, so be very stingy with water or slip.

At this point, if I can do it without messing up a texture or thinning the clay, I groom the seam area, making it as invisible as possible, which helps with finishing later. To do this, I blend the clay using the tools best suited to the job—perhaps the end of my finger, my fingernail, or one of the small rubber-tipped tools. It usually takes a combination of procedures to make the seam disappear. You might have to caulk with a spatula or add more clay to build up a texture, or you may have to remove some clay with a knife or smooth it with a rubber tool. It may also be necessary to reproduce or continue the texture over the seams. If you can't groom the seam at this time, wait until it's dry to do it.

When joining dry pieces of clay, I like to prime the joint area with a little water on my paintbrush and then add the slip. The excess slip is relatively easy to chip off after it dries.

When the joints have dried, it's time to fill in any gaps, unevenness, or anything that prevents the seam from meeting perfectly with clay. *Always use clay—not slip—to fill a gap.* Use clay to accomplish this step because slip contains too much water and any gap will only reappear when the water evaporates out of the slip. (This is also the way I fill in any cracks I find in my dry clay piece.)

Joining Fired Elements

Previously fired pieces of metal clay can certainly be attached to one another. Simply wet the appropriate areas, add thick slip, join, dry, clean the excess slip away, and refire. Always use a generous amount of slip for this process.

I've had both success and failure with this method, so if possible, I always try to create some additional mechanical method for holding the pieces together. For example, using a drill bit in my flexible shaft, I drill a hole in one of the pieces so the thick slip can fill the hole and "rivet" the two pieces together. Another example of a mechanical hold is much like a bezel, where I use a syringe to pipe on a collar of metal clay to hold a previously fired element onto another.

Joining with Oil Paste

The method I most prefer for adhering two previously fired pieces together is to use a paste that has an oil base. This product is designed for joining previously fired clay only, not for unfired clay. In my experience, the oil binder nicely penetrates the fired clay and holds pieces together with very strong joints after firing.

Slip connects a seam.

Prime a seam with water before adding slip.

You can buy this product or make it yourself.

To connect previously fired pieces, it may be necessary to run them through a quick firing (by bringing the kiln up to 1000°F [537.8°C]) to clean the surface completely of patina, grease, pencil marks, glue, and other dirt. (Anything that isn't metal clay will prevent adhesion of the paste.) Connect the two pieces with paste, let it dry, and refire according to the firing schedules of the paste or the clay with which you made the oil mixture.

Attaching Syringe Clay

When I apply syringe clay as a decorative element, I always prime the surface with a bit of water first. Putting too much water on the surface to be decorated will cause the extruded clay to slide around and not take hold, so find a happy medium.

After finishing the syringe work, I carefully touch the tip of a paintbrush dipped in water to all the joints of the syringe work. Capillary attraction seeps the water into the seam area and adds that extra bit of gluing action to help hold the syringe pieces on. Otherwise, the bits of syringe want to pop off before firing, and even after firing. Again, don't overdo the amount of water on this procedure or your syringe design/ texture will be compromised. As a final bit of insurance, I sometimes caulk the seam between the dry syringe work and the base it's connected to with clay.

When the syringe is dry, caulking the seam with clay ensures good adhesion.

Bronze Metal Clay

A formulation of copper and tin (about 90/10) mixed with water and binder, bronze clay models, textures, and works in generally the same fashion as the noble metal clays. When connecting two unfired pieces, it's necessary to score each joint surface, permeate with water, add slip, and then hold the pieces together until a seal is formed. Caulk generous amounts of clay into the seams after they're firmly attached.

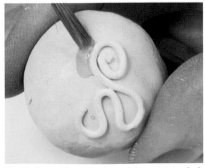
Flood the syringe design with water to help the connection.

DRY WORK

Some objects made of metal clay can be executed and finished while the clay is still in the wet stage. However, the vast majority of pieces will be more easily constructed by working alternately in the wet *and* dry stages. In other words, you'll make a component with wet clay, dry it, and then refine the piece when the clay is in the dry state, repeating this as needed to complete the piece before firing. You'll find this becomes a routine practice in your metal clay work. Sometimes, though, it's easier to construct the piece using components made of dry clay. The ease of handling because of the rigidity makes certain forms possible that would be a nightmare to try with wet clay.

Some examples of dry work include sanding, drilling, carving, scoring, and construction. These procedures are much easier to accomplish with dry, rigid clay that's able to withstand pressure without the distortion you experience with wet clay. Dry work is an essential procedure in practically all the work I do in metal clay.

Making Holes

Drill bits allow you to cut perfect holes in dry clay. They can be made of many different types of steel, but inexpensive bits are perfectly fine to use. The smallest bit I use is a #60 and the largest might go up to a #30. You can often find drill bit sets in the bargain bin at home improvement or hardware stores. I mount them in a pin vise (see page 14).

Drilling through dry clay is quite easy if you follow a few rules.

1. Make a mark with a pencil where you want the hole to go.

2. Use the pointy end of a craft knife to make a little nick or groove on the mark. This slight depression on the surface of the dry clay helps keep the bit in place as you drill.

3. With the table surface under the dry clay or a finger supporting the piece, start slowly and carefully drilling a #60 hole. This small bit drills a guide hole, which makes it much easier if you need to continue and drill a larger hole with a larger bit. Support the piece to prevent any undue pressure on the clay, which

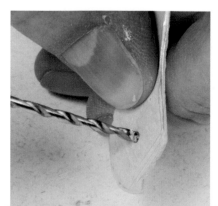

might cause breakage. Drill bits chip away the dry clay by rotating in a clockwise direction, so turn bits the correct way.

After drilling, always check to see whether there are any ragged edges left. They can be carved away by a little swipe with your craft knife.

An alternative to drilling is to use a sharp craft knife blade.

1. Begin by putting a nick into the clay at the spot where you want to make a hole.

2. Place the point of the blade in the nick, perpendicular to the surface of the clay, and twirl the knife handle while supporting the clay piece. The sharp edge of the blade will carve into the dry clay and make a round hole.

Because the blade is a triangular shape, you can make holes in all sorts of sizes.

Scraping

Sometimes an area on your dried metal clay can be addressed by scraping away clay. Use craft knives for this; both the blade and the non-blade side will work. Any other kind of tool with a sharp edge can be employed in scraping, too, such as gravers, mini chisels, and ceramic tools designed for sgraffito work.

Carving

Carving, whether decorative or corrective, is best done when the clay is bone dry. My favorite tools for this are V- and U-shaped gouges used by makers of miniature woodcarvings. The #1 liner linoleum-carving tool is also a dependable implement for this purpose.

When carving with these gouges or the linoleum tool, either raise the clay above the table surface on a piece of wood or bring the clay to the edge of the table surface. Positioning the carving hand *below* the surface of the clay puts the tool at the correct angle for optimum carving. If the angle between the tool and the surface of the clay is too great, it's difficult to carve.

Traditional metalworking tools such as gravers can work as carvers; so can miniature chisels, which I've found at various art supply stores. If you have a flexible shaft tool or a hand-held rotary tool, you can insert metal cutting burs into it to carve dry metal clay. When using mechanical tools, good support of the piece and a gentle touch with the burs will ensure the best results.

Cutting and Scoring

Cutting through wet clay is an easy procedure, but sometimes it's more advantageous to cut dry clay. If the clay is flat and you need to cut a straight line, scoring is a simple way to achieve this.

1. Place a straight edge on top of the clay and, while pressing lightly on it, draw a craft knife lightly along the edge. Your goal is not to cut all the way through the dry clay, but to cut a shallow groove.

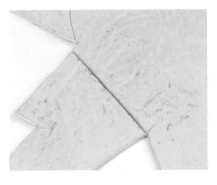

2. Grasp the clay on both sides of the groove and snap the piece in two along the incised line.

This is a very clean, easy way to cut dry clay. I've also used this method to cut curved lines by snapping off small pieces, bit by bit.

A Word about Tool Marks

When using any of the dry working tools, it's good craftsmanship to always take a critical, close-up look at every surface of the metal clay piece to make sure all indications and vestiges of the tools are gone. For example, if you've used an emery board to file away a ragged edge, check that edge and remove all the coarse file marks by using finer

and finer emeries in sequence until the edge looks consistent with the appearance of the rest of the piece.

Tool marks should disappear unless, aesthetically, they intentionally match the rest of the piece. Let's say you've fashioned a piece with an integral texture you've made using a coarse emery file. It might then be appropriate to leave those coarse marks on an edge whose shape you've refined with the emery board.

Bronze Metal Clay

When dry, bronze clay is much more resistant to abrasion than silver and gold clay are. To remove lots of material, start with the coarsest emery and use the finer grades in sequence. Excess can also be carved away with craft knives.

FIRING

Each type of clay has a time and a temperature that ensures full *sintering* of the clay. Sintering refers to the method of forming a solid object from a powdered metal by heating the object a bit below the melting point of the powder. You must reach certain temperatures and hold them for specific time periods to accomplish the interconnection between the tiny, powdered particles of metal. No matter which brand of metal clay you're working with, you should check the enclosed literature and make note of its firing schedule. (In case you misplace it, page 29 contains a firing chart for various types of metal clay.)

If you're implanting an object or a substance into your metal clay with the goal of firing it in place, make sure you know which firing schedule that object will tolerate. For example, a CZ gemstone in metal clay will fire successfully at any time and temperature, but a natural peridot will only work in the lowest-firing clay.

There are a number of ways to sinter metal clay. Torch firing and kilns (both electric and fuel powered) are the most common choices. Personally, I torch fire pieces on occasion, but normally I use a kiln that's—conveniently—designed for use with metal clay. Most metal clay artists eventually own a kiln because it's the most versatile and dependable way to sinter a piece.

If you already own a kiln that you might like to use for metal clay, make sure it heats

efficiently and in a timely manner. The large kilns used for ceramics are not well suited to metal clay because they're not always accurate in temperature and take a really long time to heat up. Smaller kilns are usually better. If you have an old enameling kiln, it could be useful. Just make sure the reading on the pyrometer is accurate.

Kiln Firing

With metal clay, you have a lot of leeway in firing. Simply pay attention to the crucial temperatures (lowest and highest) and to any implants that may be in your piece and you will have success. Once your piece is bone dry and you know the firing schedules of the different clays, it's a simple matter to fire correctly.

Supporting the Work. Never fire a metal clay piece on the floor of a kiln. Instead, place a kiln shelf directly in the kiln's bottom, supporting it on four little ceramic "feet." This way, when you insert a tool to remove the hot shelf after firing, you'll be able to grab it easily. Little feet and shelves can be obtained from any ceramic, jewelry, or metal clay supplier.

Flat kiln shelves are the best surface for firing flat pieces. I support and

nestle non-flat metal clay pieces, such as round beads, in containers filled with vermiculite or kitty litter. For this purpose, I use small stainless steel cups because they don't break down easily with firing after firing. These can be found at kitchen shops in capacities ranging from about 1/4 cup (62.5 ml) to 2 cups (500 ml).

Another choice for a container is a ceramic crucible. These small dishes are designed to hold melted metal and can withstand temperatures up to 2800°F (1537.8°C). They last for many, many firings. You can use the terra-cotta saucers placed under flowerpots for firing as well. They tend to crack easily and don't last very long, but the cost is very reasonable.

I like to use vermiculite to cushion and support contoured pieces during firing. It's a nontoxic soil conditioner and can be found at garden supply stores. You can use it over and over again, but a dust mask is necessary when working with it. Pure clay kitty litter can also be used in this capacity. If desired, you can simply mound vermiculite or kitty litter on a kiln shelf.

Another way to support a non-flat piece is with fiber blanket, a material used in the glass-fusing world. It adapts to various contours and can be

Firing Schedules for Metal Clay

Original PMC
- 1650°F (898.9°C) for two hours

PMC+
- 1650°F (898.9°C) for 10 minutes
- or 1560°F (848.9°C) for 20 minutes
- or 1470°F (798.9°C) for 40 minutes

PMC3
- 1290°F (698.9°C) for 10 minutes
- or 1200°F (648.9°C) for 20 minutes
- or 1110°F (598.9°C) for 45 minutes

PMC Gold (22-karat yellow gold)
- 1290°F (698.9°C) for 90 minutes
- or 1380°F (748.9°C) for 60 minutes
- or 1560°F (848.9°C) for 30 minutes
- or 1650°F (898.9°C) for 10 minutes

Art Clay Silver
- 1472°F (800°C) for 30 minutes
- or 1600°F (871.1°C) for 10 minutes

Art Clay 650 Low Fire
- 1200°F (648.9°C) for 30 minutes
- or 1290°F (698.9°C) for 15 minutes
- or 1380°F (748.9°C) for 10 minutes

Art Clay 650 Slow Dry
- 1200°F (648.9°C) for 30 minutes
- or 1290°F (698.9°C) for 15 minutes
- or 1380°F (748.9°C) for 10 minutes
- or 1472°F (800°C) for 5 minutes

Art Clay Gold
- 1830°F (998.9°C) for 60 minutes

Bronze Metal Clay
- Ramp kiln 250°F (121.1°C) per hour until it's 1550°F (843.3°C). Hold at 1525°F (829.4°C) for three hours, for a total firing time of 9 hours.

used a number of times before it becomes brittle. It's best to work with a dust mask when using fiber blanket.

Arranging Pieces in the Kiln.

You can fire many pieces in the kiln at the same time, but be sure to follow a few guidelines.

If you have contact between pieces in the kiln, they generally won't fuse together because the shrinkage will draw them away from each other. They can be arranged very closely, but it's a good idea to keep them from touching each other.

With the aid of little ceramic feet, you can stack shelves in your kiln. I try not to stack so many that the

interior of the kiln is completely filled. This tends to create uneven heating, which can result in both underfiring and overfiring in the same kiln load. Also, be aware that the back corners of a kiln are sometimes hot spots, so avoid placing pieces in those positions of extreme temperature.

Flat pieces on the shelf and shaped pieces supported by any method can all be fired together (see photo at top), even on the same shelf. If I'm firing a lot of beads, I place them in a large stainless steel bowl of vermiculite and put that on a shelf.

I sometimes have more than one firing schedule in the kiln at one time. When that's the case, I fire for the lowest temperature/time first, pull out the appropriate piece when done, and continue firing for the rest of the kiln load. It's also perfectly acceptable to reprogram the kiln after removing a piece.

Torch Firing

You can sinter a relatively small piece made of low-temperature firing metal clay with almost any kind of torch. Many people find the small butane torches sold in home improvement stores and kitchen stores (those torches are for preparing crème brulée—yum!) very suitable and convenient for this procedure.

I wouldn't torch fire a piece bigger than a large coin (say, 1⅝ inches [4 cm] in diameter) or with more mass than 27 grams. Nor is it practical to torch fire clay that requires firings of 2 hours at 1650°F (898.9°C). Bottom line: stick with lower temperature clays for torch firing. By the way, implanted glass is *not* suitable for torch firing.

1. Place the piece on a fireproof surface such as a soldering block, a kiln shelf, or a piece of fiber blanket.

2. Bring the piece up to a medium red glow and hold at that temperature for 3 to 5 minutes while gently rotating the torch on the metal clay.

Synthetic stones can be torch fired, but be sure not to quench the metal clay piece by putting it in water after torching—a sudden change in temperature can make stones crack, so let them slowly air cool, please.

Firing Bronze Clay

When firing bronze clay, you *must* bury it in granular, activated carbon during the firing process. The purpose of doing so is to absorb oxygen during the firing so that the microscopic particles of metal can be successfully sintered. Hold the carbon and bronze clay pieces in a covered stainless steel container in the kiln.

Depending on the type of carbon used to bury the pieces, different colorations result. If the carbon is derived from coconut, an iridescence occurs. Unfortunately, this array of teals and blues is unstable. If the carbon has been treated with silver nitrate (such as aquarium filter carbon or it's coconut-based carbon), no iridescence will result. Read the label when you buy the carbon to make sure it's not acid washed.

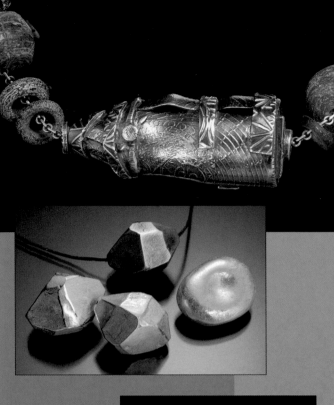

TOP
LINDA KAYE-MOSES
Draped Taper, 2007
50 cm long
Fine silver, sterling silver, antique glass beads; carved, draped, patinated
PHOTO BY EVAN J. SOLDINGER

CENTER
TIM MCCREIGHT
Untitled, 2006
Widest, 2 cm
Fine silver; molded
PHOTO BY ROBERT DIAMANTE

BOTTOM
HATTIE SANDERSON
Spinner Ring, 2006
33 x 22 x 22 cm
Fine silver
PHOTO BY ARTIST

FINISHING

When you remove a metal clay piece from the kiln, it has a pearly white appearance if it's silver, a dull yellow ocher appearance if it's gold, or a dull brown or iridescent surface if it's bronze. You're seeing the microscopic protrusions of the crystalline structure, so the appearance of the freshly fired clay doesn't resemble the surfaces we're used to seeing with metal. To achieve that shiny, mirror finish—or a satiny appearance or an aged, antique look—we have to subject the surface to some finishing processes. The finishing procedures are the same for all types of metal clay.

I think it's important to note here that the surface finishing of your metal clay piece actually begins in the dry state stage of fabrication. *The majority of the finishing work is done prior to firing.* I try to anticipate what kind of finish I'll want on the piece and do all I can to the dry surface of the clay to facilitate that end. By using emery, files, micropolishing papers, baby wipes, damp brushes, or whatever technique necessary, I give the surface of the dried metal clay a treatment that will require only a very small effort to finish after the piece is fired. It's hardly ever necessary to use traditional metalworking techniques to finish fired metal clay.

Basically, there are two extremes of finish on metal: a mirror finish and an intentionally highly scratched surface. Mirror finish means the most highly reflective and scratch-free surface that can be achieved. A scratched finish, on the other hand, consists of multiple depressions in the surface that cause light to be trapped and not bounce directly back at our eyes, so that we read the surface of the metal as matte rather than shiny. In metal clay, we can achieve both of these finishes as well as an infinite number of states in between.

In finishing the surface of any material, whether granite, oak, or either unfired or fired metal clay, you usually follow a specific sequence of steps. Begin by observing your material and you'll notice a certain state of surface scratches, the highs and lows left by the tools used to create the piece. Then find an abrasive to remove those scratches and replace them with finer scratches. Continue using successively finer abrasives until you achieve the look you desire. For example, if you want a highly polished surface, go through many steps until the scratches are invisible to the unaided eye. Usually I use successive grades of emery paper from coarse (320 grit) to fine (400 grit), which will smooth the surface of the unfired clay to prepare it for a high polish when fired.

Mirror Finish

To get a mirror finish on metal clay, it's important to take a critical look, with magnification, at the surface of your pre-fired, dried piece. Now's the time to obliterate any evidence of tools, such as the edge cut with a craft knife or the marks of an emery file. If you have a large, non-textured surface, look for scratches, nicks, or gouges, then take whatever steps necessary to make the surface completely scratch free. You can do this by caulking large gouges or smoothing scratches off with polishing paper.

If you have an area of texture, be sure to leave it alone so the texture remains crisp and clear. Textured surfaces are usually not highly polished anyway, because that finish detracts from rather than enhances the texture.

Once you're satisfied with the finish on your dry piece, fire it. After taking it out of the kiln, you have two options: hand polishing or mechanical polishing. Mechanical polishing isn't achieved with the buffing machines metalworkers use, but in a rotary, vibratory, or magnetic tumbler. These machines have a tub for holding small pieces of stainless steel called shot, the burnishing compound (an essential liquid that aids the burnishing process), and the work to be polished. As your metal clay piece tumbles around inside, the constant motion of the tub and the shot impact it

FAR LEFT
Scratched finish
LEFT
Mirror finish

thousands of times. The little pieces of steel act like tiny burnishers, rubbing the surface of the metal clay to result in a shiny, bright finish.

I use a small rotary tumbler whose barrel contains about 2 pounds (0.9 kg) of stainless steel mixed shot and about 2 cups (0.5 l) of burnishing compound. I tumble a piece for about 30 minutes, open up, and check the progress. Two hours in the tumbler will give a bright mirror finish.

If you're tumbling a bead or a hollow object that has holes, plug up the holes or the shot will accumulate inside the hollow form. I thread copper wire through the bead holes to prevent the shot from entering. If steel shot should get inside a bead, shake it, and it will usually come out.

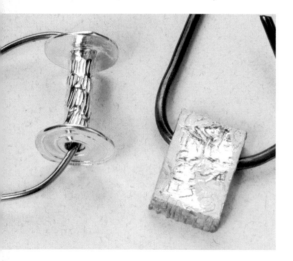

If the bead's really plugged up, empty the tumbler, fill it halfway with water, and drop the bead in. Tumble it this way until all the shot empties from the bead.

Hand polishing is best achieved by using a jeweler's burnisher. Use these highly polished pieces of steel to rub and compact the surface of the fired metal clay. The surfaces of fine silver

and fine gold move and flatten easily, so the hand-polishing process is quite easy and quick. Get a firm grip on the metal clay piece and rub with a good degree of firmness to achieve a mirror finish. The pointed end of the burnisher allows access to small areas.

Another way to achieve a highly polished surface is to use the micro-polishing papers in sequence, starting with the coarsest and ending with the finest. You'll be amazed at the beautiful surface you can get with this technique. Using your fingers as support for the papers is perfectly fine, but sometimes wrapping the papers around a rigid form, such as a craft stick, gives you a little more leverage to speed up the process.

Mechanical buffing machines are not a good method for polishing metal clay. The porous metal clay traps the greasy buffing compounds and results in a less than desirable surface. I would never use traditional mechanical buffing procedures on metal clay when the other methods I've explained are so easy to accomplish.

Satin or Scratched Finish

The surface of your metal clay can be covered with consistent scratches to achieve a softer, more matte finish. I prefer this finish when my pieces have textured surfaces. Texture doesn't read very well when all parts of the surfaces are highly polished, because the eye has a hard time sorting out the highs and lows. When the surface is less reflective, it's easier to distinguish the relief.

Again, I'll discuss the metal clay piece in its dry, unfired state: this is when the preparation for a scratched surface begins. Make a close

assessment to check for big gouges or inconsistencies in the surface of the piece. Fix them now. If I'm planning to use a brass/steel brush, pumice, steel wool, or polishing paper for a finish, I make the surface of the dry clay as smooth and flawless as possible and then brush the surface after firing.

Once the piece has the desired scratched surface, fire it. After firing, bring out the reflective quality of the metal by repeating the surface treatment you applied prior to firing.

Here are some choices of abrasives that give a scratched finish. I list them approximating the sequence from coarsest, which gives the brightest scratched surface, to finest, which results in a softer appearance.

- Emery or abrasive paper, about 320 grit
- Green kitchen scrub pad
- Steel brush (use with soapy water)*
- Emery paper, 400 grit
- Brass brush (use with soapy water)*
- Emery paper, 600 grit
- 0000 steel wool (use with water)*
- Powdered pumice (use with water)*
- Polishing paper, 1200 grit*

*Use these after firing

Steel and brass brushes have more of a burnishing action than an abrasive one. (Abrasion means that material is actually removed.) When you use pumice or emery, you're removing small amounts of metal clay.

If you apply any of the above materials to a freshly fired piece, a certain amount of burnishing will occur to compact the surface of the metal clay. The result will vary according to the amount of relief or texture on the surface and the amount of pressure you apply as you rub. All these materials require some experimentation to see what you like about each finish.

When using steel wool and powdered pumice for a finish, always lubricate with water. It seems to make the process more efficient and successful. When using steel and brass brushes, apply liquid soap to the bristles and brush your piece, dipping the brush frequently in water for lubrication. If you use a brass brush dry, it will leave behind a fine deposit of brass on the silver surface, which imparts an undesirable yellowish tinge.

Combining Finishes

All of the aforementioned finishing procedures can be used in combination. For instance, to create one of my favorite finishes for a textured surface, I brush vigorously with a brass brush and soapy water, then take my steel burnisher and rub it firmly over the high spots of the texture to brighten them. The result is a frosty, sparkly surface.

Blackening Silver and Gold

To oxidize (or patina) silver, gold, and bronze means to use chemicals to blacken the metal. Oxidizing the metal can refer to anything from a completely blackened appearance to a lightly darkened effect in just the recesses of the textures. Patina emphasizes texture, somewhat softens the piece, and gives it an antique look.

Two chemicals are used for patina: liver of sulfur (an alchemical term for sulfurated potash) and commercial blackeners, which contain dilute hydrochloric acid. Liver of sulfur turns silver black but has no effect on gold, whereas commercial patinas will blacken gold. This is important to know in the case of kum boo or any bimetal creation, when you don't wish to oxidize the gold but do want to oxidize the silver.

If I know I want my final finish to have a black patina, I usually apply the chemical to freshly fired clay. I feel that the tooth of the white, crystalline structure gives the most depth to the application of the chemical. The patina chemicals can certainly be applied to mirror-finished metal or brushed metal without a problem, so it's no tragedy to change your mind about a finish. In that vein, if you apply a patina chemical and don't like the way it looks, simply burn it off by heating gently with a torch or placing it in a 1200°F (648.9°C) kiln for a few minutes. Your silver piece will return to a white finish and you can start again.

Patina the piece by dipping or brushing the chemical on and then removing the excess black areas with an abrasive to create a contrast between the dark parts in the recesses and the exposed metal areas in the protruding parts of the texture. How much to take off depends on the look you're trying to achieve. The means you use to remove the patina will also have an effect on the look of the piece. For example, if you use a brass brush to remove the black, the fine wires of the brush will reach into lots of nooks and crannies and much of the patina will be removed. On the other hand, if you moisten the tips of your fingers, dip them into powdered pumice, and rub the high spots of the texture, you'll remove far less.

Liver of Sulfur. Liver of sulfur is sold in dry, pellet form. Its potency is very easily weakened by exposure to sunlight and air, so after purchase, store it in a well-sealed dark container stored, in turn, in plastic bags in a cupboard. To make a solution, dissolve a pea-size pebble of the dry material in 1 cup (250 ml) of water heated to just below the simmering point. Use this only in a well-ventilated area. Immerse your metal clay piece in the solution until you're satisfied with the results, take it out with tweezers, and rinse it in cold water.

By lowering the temperature of the liver of sulfur solution, you can achieve various colors of the spectrum, such as gold, blue, and magenta, on your silver. These colors don't last forever because of the natural tendency of the metal to continue to blacken. To prolong the colors, some people seal the surface with a microcrystalline wax or with a spray acrylic fixative.

Commercial Blackeners. To use commercial chemicals, simply dip the entire piece or paint the chemical on selected areas with a brush.

If steel comes in contact with these chemicals, they can be contaminated and become ineffective, so I use cheap, kid's paintbrushes that have all-plastic handles. Leave the blackener on as long as directed by the manufacturer, then rinse the piece with cold water to stop the chemical action. The same removal procedures as those with liver of sulfur take place at this stage.

Colored-Pencil Application

It's possible to get almost any color onto the surface of metal clay by using wax-based colored pencils. The piece needs to be freshly fired with nothing done to the white surface. Apply the pencils in solid areas or overlap and blend colors; do whatever you like.

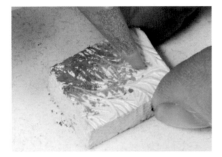

A small amount of turpentine on a cotton swab takes off excess pencil and blends the colors.

Set the wax-based color into the surface of the metal by leaving the piece on a cup warmer for a short time.

At this point you can lightly scratch with a brass brush, or use steel wool or pumice to take the pencil off the high points of the metal. You can burnish the metal as well. Let it dry, if necessary, then spray on a light coating of acrylic fixative to stabilize the color.

How you choose a finish for your piece is based on your own trial and error and subjective decisions. There is no wrong finish, only an inconsistent, poorly executed one. A single piece might look good with any one of a number of surface treatments. Finish choices are endless, so have fun and experiment!

TIM MCCREIGHT
Untitled, 2006
1.5 cm wide
Fine silver
PHOTO BY ROBERT DIAMANTE

ROBYN A. KRUTCH
The One That Got Away, 2006
6 x 8 x 0.5 cm
Metal clay, cork clay; embossed, carved
PHOTO BY TAMI MEADER PHOTOGRAPHY

LORA HART
Untitled, 2007
2.9 x 2.9 x 1.6 cm
Metal clay, sterling silver,
aquamarine, black pearl;
hand formed, fabricated,
oxidized
PHOTO BY MARSHA THOMAS

LORA HART
Three Beads, 2006
2.9 x 1.7 x 0.3 cm
Metal clay, sterling silver; kum
boo, hand formed, fabricated,
oxidized
PHOTO BY MARSHA THOMAS

ADDING STONES, GLASS & MORE

SETTING STONES

When we think of jewelry, gems and gemlike materials naturally come to mind. By adding these to our metal clay, we can introduce color, focus attention on a particular area, or add a subtle accent.

Selecting Gemstones

Before getting to the mechanics of stone setting, it's important to touch on the topic of gemstones. Three types of laboratory-grown gems are safe to fire in all types of metal clay: corundum (ruby and sapphire), spinel, and cubic zirconia (CZ). It's always good to ask the vendor if the gems are suitable for firing in metal clay.

Purchase stones from reputable gem purveyors who will accurately identify the chemical makeup of the gem. Otherwise, you may not have a good idea what you're purchasing. Any good gem dealer will be more than happy to give specifics about the material for sale. The term *laboratory-grown corundum*, for example, is more descriptive than the term *synthetic sapphire*.

Natural gemstones are mostly off-limits with metal clay because they can't withstand the temperatures and the duration of the firing schedules. Some notable exceptions are peridot and garnet, which are safe to use with metal clay that fires at 1110°F (598.9°C) for 45 minutes. When planning to implant gemstones in bronze clay, keep in mind that they must be able to withstand metal clay's nine-hour firing schedule. Information about which gemstones are usable is available from jewelers' supply catalogs and other sources on the Internet, or refer to the list on page 38.

Natural gems that can't be fired can become a part of a metal clay design by attaching them after firing. I'll discuss some solutions for this further on.

GEMS SUITABLE FOR FIRING

Fast Ramping (1110°F [598.9°C] for 30 minutes)

- Chrome Diopside
- Garnet (Almandine, Pyrope, Rhodolite, Tsavorite)
- Hematite
- Moonstone
- Peridot
- Sapphire (Black star)
- Synthetic Alexandrite
- Synthetic emerald
- Synthetic ruby
- Synthetic sapphire
- Synthetic spinel
- CZ

These stones have given iffy results with fast ramping. Try them if you don't mind taking risks!

- Tavalite CZ
- Tourmaline
- Synthetic star corundum

Slow Ramping (ramped 500°F [260°C] per hour to reach 1110°F [598.9°C], then held for 30 minutes)

- Tanzanite
- Topaz (green, white)
- Tourmaline (green)

With slow ramping, these stones have shown dicey results. If you feel like taking a gamble, you can set them in metal clay.

- Aquamarine
- Labradorite
- Moonstone (peach, rainbow, silver)

Torching

- CZ (green, white)
- Lab-grown garnet (green)
- Lab-grown moissanite
- Lab-grown sapphire (white)
- Lab-grown spinel (blue)
- Labradorite
- Moonstone (peach, silver)
- Peridot
- Rhodolite
- Ruby (A- and AAA-grades)
- Sapphire (blue A- and AAA-grades; white)
- Tanzanite

Courtesy of Kevin Whitmore and the Bell Group, Inc.

GEMS TO AVOID

- Agate (Cameo)
- Aquamarine
- Aventurine
- Carnelian
- Chalcedony
- Citrine
- Diamond
- Emerald
- Fire opal
- Iolite
- Jadeite
- Lapis (denim, lazuli)
- Malachite
- Onyx (Black)
- Pyrite
- Quartz (rose, rutilated, smoky)
- Rhodochrosite
- Tourmaline (pink)
- Topaz
- Turquoise

Basic Stone-Setting Guidelines

Whether you're working with metal or metal clay, the guidelines for setting stones are quite similar.

- The stone must be completely secure and must not wiggle.

- The stone must not be tilted in the setting.

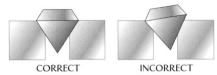

CORRECT   INCORRECT

- The stone must be visible and not overly covered up by the mechanism securing it.

- If faceted, the culet—the pointed, bottom end of the stone—must be contained within the design so it doesn't poke the wearer.

CORRECT   INCORRECT

- The backing of a faceted stone and most cabochon stones should be open to make the piece lightweight and allow light to show from the back.

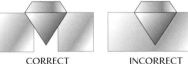

CORRECT   INCORRECT

- Special to metal clay: In certain settings, the unfired metal clay must be at least as high, if not a tad higher, than the top of the stone. If the stone isn't set below the metal

CORRECT   INCORRECT

clay, it could pop out of its setting because the clay shrinks during firing. By setting it below the level of the clay, we compensate for the shrinkage, keeping the stone securely in the perfect position.

Once you've fulfilled these dos and don'ts, you need follow no other rules. Aesthetics can be your guide. There are far too many ways to set a stone for us to explore here, so I'll describe just a few of the popular ways for setting stones in metal clay. Your experimentation will yield more possibilities.

Simple Insertion Setting

The simplest way to set stones is to push the gem into wet clay. A couple of conditions must be met before insertion.

- You must have an ample amount of clay so the stone can be pushed far enough down so the table or top of the stone is even or a bit below the level of the clay.

- With a high-domed cabochon, it's not always necessary to push the stone down to the level of the top of the dome. If the stone is a faceted one, there must be enough clay so that the culet isn't sticking out.

- Sufficient clay must surround the stone so that when shrinkage takes place during the firing, no breaks or cracks will form in the collar that encircles the gem. Bigger stones need thicker collars than small stones.

- An opening should be cut into the clay before inserting the stone so that the back of the stone is exposed.

If all these criteria are met, then the rest of the configuration of the stone setting and the piece is a matter of the maker's personal choice.

Extruded Collar Setting

The other method of setting stones employs the syringe to extrude a collar of clay around a stone.

The size of the stone dictates the diameter of the extruded clay. The larger the stone, the larger the collar needs to be. If you have a stone with a widest dimension of less than 4 mm, a collar with a diameter of 1 millimeter should hold it very well. If your stone is between 4 mm and 8 mm, a 2-millimeter collar will work. Really big stones 20 mm or larger may require many layers and applications of extruded clay to bolster the thickness of the collar. When doing this, after each round of extrusion I blend in the coil with a paintbrush and water. (You could also hand roll a worm of the right thickness to go around a big stone and dispense with the syringe altogether.)

For a flat-bottomed cabochon, the extruded clay should be laid down to connect with the base of the piece and to overlap the angle of the stone. If making a syringe setting for a faceted stone, the girdle of the stone must sit flush with the surrounding clay. The girdle of the stone is the outermost dimension of the stone. You can set the girdle even with the surface of the clay in one of two ways.

Setting in Wet Clay

1. Once you've established where the stone is going to sit, cut a guide hole through all the thicknesses of clay. I like to use a plastic straw with the appropriate diameter to do this. Choose a size to make a hole that won't allow the stone to fall through. This allows the culet of the stone to be exposed.

2. Carefully press the stone into the hole until the girdle is flush with the surrounding clay, making sure the stone isn't cockeyed.

3. Pipe a coil of syringe clay around the stone so the coil touches the base clay and also overlaps the top angle (crown) of the stone.

4. Blend the ends of the wire together to give a seamless look. You can do this when the wire is wet or dry; you decide which is best.

5. After the setting is dry, check to make sure there's a good connection between the coil and the base clay. If you see gaps or cracks, fill them in.

Setting in Dry Clay

1. Drill a hole smaller than the greatest dimension of the stone.

2. To allow for the angle between the girdle and the pavilion—the stone's base—you need to remove some of the dried clay around the drill hole. This allows the girdle to sit flush with the clay. Remove the excess clay with a craft knife held at an angle.

If you're working with a brilliant-cut or a round stone and you happen to have stone-setting burs in your toolbox, you can use them.

3. Seat the girdle of the stone flush, then extrude the syringe clay to connect with the base and overlap the top angle (crown) of the stone.

4. Make sure the connecting ends of the extruded coil are seamless. Do this either wet by blending with a paintbrush or dry by caulking with clay and filing away excess clay.

5. After the setting is dry, check that you have a good connection between the coil and the base clay. If there are gaps or cracks, fill them in.

Commercial stone-setting burs for brilliant-cut faceted stones

Mock Prong Setting

A variation of the previous setting is to add mock prongs rather than a collar of extruded syringe clay. I call them mock prongs because you don't actually bend them over a stone, but instead position small bits of clay that are then fired over the stone to hold it in the way traditional prongs do. Syringe clay is the most convenient way to create these prongs, but you can make them other ways, too.

Position the girdle of the stone flush with the surface of the clay, or set the cabochon flat on the surface. Pipe at least three equidistant prongs on top of the stone and connect them with the base clay, positioning them so the stone can't fall out once the clay is dry. You might look at jewelry-making books to study traditional prong positioning.

Removing Clay from Stone Surfaces

No matter which method you choose to set and fire a stone in metal clay, it's very important to remove any clay that has dried on the surface of the stone. If you don't remove it from the stone, it can fuse to the gem and mar its surface. To remove this excess clay, I use a stiff paintbrush to carefully flick any clay off the top and the bottom of the stone.

You can also use a small paintbrush dipped in alcohol to remove any clay on the surface of the stone. Just be careful not to blend the alcohol with the surrounding clay and create more "slip" on top of the stone.

On the underside of the setting, it's sometimes necessary to use a craft knife to delicately carve away any excess clay that will obscure the stone and also open up the back of the setting.

Setting Items After Firing Metal Clay

Objects that can't be fired present some interesting possibilities for creative settings. These might be crystals or pebbles, or you could cast your net even wider to set pieces of wood and other found objects. To set anything after firing the clay, you must reserve a place for it before the metal clay goes into the kiln.

Every item has a footprint. With a cabochon, it's the outline of the stone, which could be an oval, a circle, or any freeform shape. In the case of a faceted stone, it's the shape from the girdle to the culet. Once you've determined the footprint, you will make a clone.

Use only low-shrinkage metal clays for this technique. My clone material of choice is paper clay because it's easily formed and unaffected by high firing temperatures. The clone won't burn up or shrink during the firing process, thereby reserving a place the exact size and shape of your cabochon. After firing, the paper clay is easily chipped out.

1. Photocopy the cabochon, or scan it and print the image.

2. Very precisely cut 1 millimeter outside the edge of the image. This is your template.

3. Roll out a sheet of paper clay about 1/8 inch (3 mm) thick. If the item you want to set is really small, it can be thinner.

4. Place the paper template on the sheet of paper clay and cut precisely around it with a craft knife.

This is the clone. Let it dry thoroughly, preventing distortion by keeping it flat and not applying heat to speed the process.

As you're creating your metal clay piece, insert the clone into the design where you eventually want to set the stone or found object. Fashion prongs or some other means of holding the object in place. (The prongs must stand straight up so you can drop the item in after firing.)

After firing, chip out the clone with a needle tool or some other pointed instrument.

With a faceted stone or any irregular object such as a crystal cluster, you first make a mold of the part of the gemstone that will eventually nestle in the metal clay, then create the clone to serve as a seat for it.

I use room-temperature vulcanizing (RTV) silicone mold material to do this. Once cured, this material is flexible and durable enough to be used repeatedly. An alternative to RTV is polymer clay, which I explain on the next page.

First, here's how to make an RTV mold.

1. RTV mold-making compound comes in two jars, part A and part B. Mix an equal ratio of both parts of sufficient size for the stone. You now have about 2 minutes of working time to shape the resulting silicone compound lump and press the stone in up to the girdle.

In the case of an irregular object, press it down into your mold material enough to make an impression but not so much that you create an undercut.

Think easy in, easy out. If some of the mold material covers a portion of the gem, you won't be able to remove the gem without destroying the mold.

2. Once the mold has cured and hardened, which takes 12 to 15 minutes, remove the stone. Because of the silicone content, your gemstone will pop right out.

3. Pack wet paper clay into the mold, all the way up to the top.

4. Give the paper clay sufficient time to dry (in the case of large amounts, this may take 24 hours or more) and remove. Paper clay must be bone dry—all the way through—before it goes into the kiln. You now have your paper clay clone to place into the metal clay design of your choice.

Follow these directions to make a mold out of polymer clay.

1. Push the object into a lump of polymer clay and carefully extract it.

2. Bake the polymer.

3. Use this polymer mold to make a paper clay clone to insert into your metal clay creation.

4. After firing, drop the stone into the footprint to see whether any adjustments need to be made. You may have to do a little grinding to get a perfect seat, for example. *Before* you insert the stone, I recommend placing 12 inches (30.5 cm) of dental floss across the seat depression. That way, you can pull on the dental floss to pop the stone out if it gets stuck!

Whether you make a mold from RTV silicone or polymer clay, remember to follow the stone-setting rules by opening the back of the stone, protecting the culet, and creating a means of holding the stone in place once the firing is complete.

Setting the Stone

After firing and finishing, the last thing to do is set your stone. If you've made prongs, gently bend them to touch the stone. Fine silver and gold are very malleable, so prongs shouldn't be hard to move. You can use a prong pusher, a bezel rocker, or any of a number of official jeweler's tools. I have a 4-inch (10.2 cm) length of hardwood for bending prongs that works quite well. A short piece of hardwood dowel or the end of a plastic toothbrush works, too. The wood can be shaped to accommodate a prong, or flattened to rock a bezel. Whatever works for you is the right tool.

We've explored the fact that certain gemstones can be implanted into metal clay and survive the firing. Glass, pieces of ceramic, and metal can also be included with some interesting and practical results.

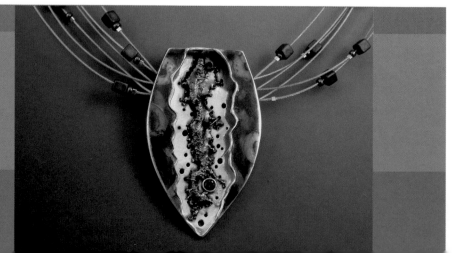

HOLLY GAGE
African Warrior Shield, 2007
5.5 x 3.4 x 5.5 cm
Metal clay, titanium, ruby, kum boo, liver of sulfur; patinated
PHOTO BY ARTIST

IMPLANTING GLASS, CERAMICS, AND METAL

Glass in Low-Fire Clay

Many people like to use the cabochon-shaped glass pieces that contain dichroic glass. Approach setting these pieces the same way you would if you were dealing with a fireable gemstone cabochon.

The clays that fire at the lowest temperatures are good candidates for use when implanting glass. With a firing time of 45 minutes at temperatures of 1110 to 1200°F (598.9 to 648.9°C), the glass isn't usually altered in shape; at these low temperatures, the glass won't fuse to the metal.

It's always best to use mechanical means to lock the glass into the metal clay. This could mean a bezel type of construction, or prongs, or clay that overlaps and holds the glass into the piece, top and bottom.

Glass in Medium-Fire Clay

Metal clay that fires around 1470°F (798.9°C) is also suitable for implanting glass. The difference between the low-fire clay and this one is that the glass may flow slightly and fuse to the metal during the firing process. When using this clay, mechanical holds aren't always required. The usual procedure is to create some sort of ring of containment with metal clay around the glass to capture it as the clay shrinks during firing. Merely setting the glass piece on top of the metal clay won't always ensure a secure connection.

I will assume your piece of glass is a cabochon or a piece of sheet that will sit flat. You can back it with clay or you can leave the back of the glass open.

1. Roll out a worm of clay that is about one-half to three-quarters the height of the cabochon or piece of glass you are setting. The coil should be longer than the circumference of the glass, very smooth, and free of blemishes or cracks. Use a bit of water on a paintbrush to smooth and hydrate the coil.

2. Wrap the worm loosely around the glass and create a lap seam. Carefully smooth and groom the seam to make it consistent with the rest of the coil. This joint needs to be strong and secure due to the stress it will bear during the shrinking that occurs when firing. If it breaks apart, it will be at the seam area or at an area that has a crack. Making sure that these areas of concern are attended to before firing will give you a successful setting.

Once this surrounding clay worm is complete, you can decorate and otherwise work on the rest of the piece.

If the back of your glass is exposed, place a piece of fireable fiber shelf paper (obtained from glass fusing suppliers), cut to size, under your piece. This will prevent the glass from fusing to the kiln shelf in case of overheating.

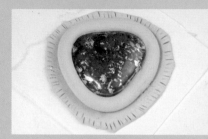

If you have a piece of glass larger than 1 inch (2.5 cm) square, it's a good idea to ramp up more slowly to the firing temperature than you normally would. Most of the metal clay kilns have a slow ramp program for just this purpose.

Once the firing schedule is completed, open the kiln door until the pyrometer reads 1000°F (537.8°C). Immediately shut the door and *do not* open it again until the kiln is at room temperature. (When I'm firing things with glass, I usually do them at the end of the day to let the kiln cool

overnight.) It's important to let the piece cool slowly from 1000°F (537.8°C) down. Cooling too fast can result in cracked glass. This technique is called "crash cooling" and it prevents **devitrification** in some types of glass. Devitrification results in a scummy surface on the glass and is not attractive.

With a piece of sheet glass, you can wrap the edges with metal clay sheet, which acts almost like a stained glass/copper foil wrapping. A bit of moisture on the glass will allow the paper to adhere nicely all the way around the perimeter. You can then connect other pieces of metal clay to the paper. Fire the piece at the recommended schedules for that particular clay and go through the gradual cooling mentioned above.

We don't always have nice flat cabochons or sheets of glass. Sometimes we want to use lumps of beach glass, broken beads, or other irregular shapes. An alternative way of setting these pieces is to employ low-firing metal clay paste. By applying a thick coating of paste to the perimeter or circumference of the glass, you can capture the piece and effectively form a locking mechanism to connect the glass to the body of the piece. Remember to make the paste layer thick enough to accommodate for shrinkage. I paint one layer, let it dry, paint a second layer, let it dry, and then add a third layer. For a piece of glass bigger than 1 inch (2.5 cm) in area, you might consider adding a fourth layer.

Ceramics

You can implant small pieces of previously fired ceramics into metal clay. Fragments of broken porcelain plates and items of that sort can be interesting in a metal clay piece. Most bits of ceramic can withstand even the highest firing temperatures. (It's always a good idea to do a test piece by placing a piece of ceramic in the kiln and running it through the firing cycle to see whether it survives.) If you use the lower-firing clays, there shouldn't be a problem.

The setting of the ceramic pieces can be achieved by any of the afore-

mentioned techniques for setting stones or glass. If your ceramic piece has a broken edge you find unattractive, painting paste over it will make it more visually acceptable.

Metal

It's logical that fine silver and fine gold can be implanted into metal clay, but what about other metals?

Sterling Silver. Sterling silver is probably the most useful metal to implant into metal clay because it allows us to make mechanisms that have the tensile strength to function as findings. It's an alloy of 92.5% fine silver and 7.5% copper. That little bit of copper adds durability to the alloy and makes it suitable for the wear and tear jump rings and clasps are prone to. Metal clay is not suitable for making these small components that require great strength. By implanting silver wire jump rings, hooks, etc. into low-firing metal clay, we can create custom findings for our creations.

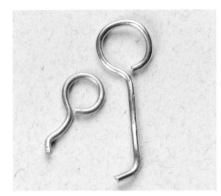

In addition to counting on the shrinkage to capture the wire, I always notch the end of, or bend slightly, any silver wire that I insert into my clay piece to ensure a mechanical hold. At temperatures in the 1100 to 1200°F (593.3 to 648.9°C) range, the silver doesn't fuse to the metal clay, so this provides a locking mechanism of some sort.

As long as you implant sterling silver into metal clay that fires below 1200°F (648.9°C), you shouldn't damage the structure of the sterling. Higher firing temperatures and a longer duration of firing time will begin to deteriorate the molecular structure of the silver and render it brittle. I prefer to use clay that fires at the lowest possible temperature, 1110°F (598.9°C), because I know the only change in the sterling will be oxidation and annealing.

Argentium. This is a relatively new silver alloy in the field of metalwork and consists of fine silver, germanium, and a tiny bit of copper. Argentium behaves much like sterling silver does as far as strength and appropriateness for findings. It doesn't oxidize to a black color when implanted in fired metal clay; the surface just dulls a little. I would fire it at the low temperatures, not beyond 1110°F (598.9°C).

An added bonus in using Argentium is heat hardening. If you place it in a 580°F (304.4°C) kiln for 45 to 60 minutes, then allow it to air cool, it increases the Argentium's hardness, which is very good for findings. If you implant a piece of Argentium, you should perform the heat-hardening procedure after firing.

Gold. Fine gold (24 karat) and 22-karat gold can be implanted in all forms of metal clay. These high karats of gold and fine silver naturally want to migrate and blend together on a molecular level when in an atmosphere of high heat. Therefore, in most cases, a secure join will occur between the two. This is the principle that we rely on for the surface decoration technique of kum boo (see the Wire Armature Bead, page 107).

Treat lower karats such as 18- or 14-karat gold in the same way as sterling silver: use lower-firing clay and a mechanical hold. The exposed surface of these lower karats will oxidize during the firing. During the finishing process, you'll need to remove this oxidation layer with abrasives.

BONNIE POLINSKI
Surf and Sky, 2007
3.7 x 1.9 cm
Ceramic bead, hollow bead, under/over glaze stains, metal clay, silver; raku-fired, hand formed, hand painted
PHOTO BY VONNA MASLANKA

Gold-Filled Wire. This is a material that's not solid gold but a thick layer of 12- or 14-karat gold bonded and laminated to a brass core. This material should also be treated like sterling silver, using lower firing temperatures. Expect oxidation to occur on the exposed metal.

Copper and Its Alloys. Copper, brass, and bronze can withstand the highest firing temperatures but will require mechanical means to lock them in place, as well as treatment to remove oxidation from exposed areas.

THIS PAGE
BARBARA BECKER SIMON
Green Rocks, 2005
Longest bead,
5.5 x 1.3 x 1.5 cm
Fine silver, glass, ceramic,
turquoise, granite, hollow box
metal clay beads; lampworked
PHOTO BY LARRY SANDERS

OPPOSITE PAGE, TOP LEFT
ABBY JOHNSTON
Untitled, 2007
3.5 x 3 cm
Fine silver, metal clay,
aura 22, lead-filled cord
PHOTO BY ARTIST

OPPOSITE PAGE, TOP RIGHT
NANCY KARPEL
Pod Bead Pendant, 2003
4.5 x 2.2 x 0.7 cm
Fine silver, 24-karat metal clay,
18-karat gold; hollow formed,
textured, pierced, soldered
PHOTO BY FRANK POOLE

OPPOSITE PAGE, BOTTOM
TERRY KOVALCIK
Painted Lentils, 2007
Largest, 3.5 cm
Fine silver clay, black onyx
beads, sterling silver, silver
paste; painted
PHOTO BY CORRIN JACOBSEN
KOVALCIK

CREATING
TEXTURE PLATES

A texture plate is a flat sheet of material that has a three-dimensional pattern or design. It can be an all-over, repetitive pattern; a specific design, image, or text; or a combination of any of these things. Metal clay takes on texture so easily and successfully that these plates are a versatile and essential item in our design "toolbox." We can roll out our clay on them to achieve texture, or impress the plate onto just portions of metal clay. We can use them over and over; another advantage of these plates lies in their durability.

You can buy rubber stamps and large texture plates of rubber that have prescribed designs. It's also possible to create your own designs drawn in high-contrast black and white and have custom-made rubber stamps and sheets made. The manufacturing company will attach the stamps to handles or leave them unmounted, as you wish.

In my quest to distill and define my own design ideas, I make my own texture plates. There are several ways of making them, and most are quite easy to do.

MOLDED TEXTURE PLATES

Often, you'll come across a texture you'd like to roll clay onto to reproduce, but something about it presents a problem. For instance, say you've found a stretch of slate that has a subtle, layered quality. If the stone is on your garden path, it will be a little inconvenient to roll clay onto it. Or with a plastic needle-point sheet, the metal clay could get stuck in the openings, so pulling off a cleanly textured metal clay sheet might be difficult.

With both of these examples, it would be best to make a mold of the slate or plastic so that the metal clay could easily be rolled onto that. I like two materials for this procedure: polymer clay and two-part silicone rubber mold material.

Polymer Clay Plates

Polymer clay is marketed under several brand names. Choose any that you like.

1. Condition the polymer clay by kneading and rolling it with your hands for 3 to 10 minutes until it has a good working consistency. Roll out a slab about eight cards thick.

2. Apply some kind of release material, such as a light dusting of cornstarch or talcum powder, or a light film of olive oil, to the surface to be molded, choosing whichever one won't damage the texture you wish to mold.

3. Place the sheet of polymer on the surface and impress the polymer evenly. You can do this with your hands or a rolling pin.

4. Lift the polymer carefully and check to see whether you got a good impression. If so, carefully remove it and bake the clay according to the directions on the package.

One disadvantage of polymer texture plates is their inflexibility; metal clay that's been rolled onto the plate must be pried off with care. Remember to clean all tools that might be shared with metal clay to avoid contamination.

Two-Part Silicone Plates

Two-part silicone mold material is available commercially from most jewelry and metal clay suppliers. It usually comes in two separate containers, each holding one part of the mold material, and each a different color for ease of mixing.

1. Take a lump of each color, making sure each is as equal in size as possible. Knead them together with your fingers for 30 to 60 seconds until you achieve a uniform color with no marbling.

Quick Reference

Unless otherwise indicated, when making textured metal clay sheets for the projects in this book, you should do the following.

1. Roll out a sheet three cards thick.

2. Apply a light amount of release agent—olive oil, solid balm, or talc in the case of rubber stamps—to the texture plate and to the clay, if necessary.

3. Roll out the metal clay sheet onto the texture plate with two cards as the spacers.

4. Carefully peel the clay from the texture plate and lay it on an acetate sheet. Cover it with plastic wrap if you want to keep it moist.

2. Apply the silicone to the surface you want to mold. You have a few minutes to work before it begins to cure.

3. Allow the silicone to cure, undisturbed, for 15 to 30 minutes. You can tell when it has cured by poking your fingernail into the edge. If you leave no impression and the silicone bounces back, the process is finished and you can peel the mold off the surface of your texture.

This compound has the advantage of self-lubrication, so you need no release agent to prevent the metal clay from sticking to the silicone mold. It's also flexible, which makes removing the metal clay quite easy. These molds last a long time and can be used over and over again, but getting an impression with them is sometimes a little tricky if the molds aren't flat. I roll out a sheet of metal clay one card thicker than I need, and then roll it onto the silicone mold or press with my fingers to get an impression.

TOP

WENDY WALLIN MALINOW
Silver Lichen, 2007
13 x 14 x 0.3 cm
Metal clay, linen; hand formed, textured, patinated
PHOTO BY COURTNEY FRISSE

BOTTOM

REBECCA SKEELS
Pollen Bead, 2007
2 x 5.5 x 1.5 cm
Metal clay; molded, hollow formed, drilled, burnished
PHOTO BY ARTIST

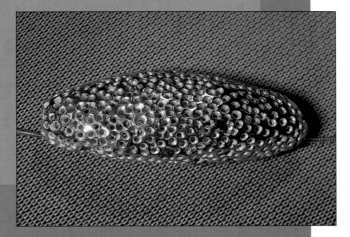

TEAR-AWAY TECHNIQUE

This is a process conceived by Gwen Gibson, a gifted polymer clay artist. In the world of polymer clay, it's used as a means of creating a low, subtle texture. Metal clay enthusiasts use it as a texture plate to make impressions of similar delicate relief. If you like to use kum-boo as an embellishing technique, metal clay surfaces with a tear-away texture are a perfect surface. (See the Wire Armature Bead on page 107.)

The basic process involves transferring an image copied on a toner-type copy machine onto the surface of unbaked polymer clay. After burnishing and setting with a little heat, peel off the paper image (hence the name tear-away); the toner that's been in contact with the polymer clay takes some of the clay with it as it's ripped off. The result is a relief where the deep parts are those that were touched by the toner, and the high parts are where only paper came in contact with it.

For best results, use Sculpey III polymer clay, and start with an image no larger than 2 x 3 inches (5.1 x 7.6 cm) until you've mastered the technique.

1. Make a black-and-white photocopy—with the black as dense as you can get it—using gloss-coated business paper on a toner copier. In creating your design, keep in mind that the white areas will be the lowest on the finished metal clay and the black areas will be the highest. Cut out the design, leaving extra paper for margins and a tab for pulling it off later.

2. Roll out the polymer clay to the thickest setting on a pasta machine, about 1/8 inch (3 mm). (A pasta machine will create a slab with the perfect flatness and consistency, but you can roll one out by hand instead using spacers.) Cut the slab, leaving ample space for the image plus at least 3/4 inch (1.9 cm) all around.

3. Place the photocopy face down on the slab and burnish it with the heel of your hand or your fist for 2 minutes.

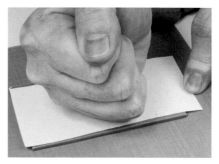

4. Put the slab under an incandescent lamp for 7 to 8 minutes, with the bulb about 6 inches (15.2 cm) away from the paper. Turn off the lamp and let the clay rest for 10 minutes. Burnish it for another minute.

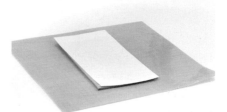

5. Place the slab back under the lamp for another 7 minutes. Hold on to the clay, grasp the paper tab, and pull low and fast in one smooth motion.

6. Bake at 265°F (129.4°C) for 20 minutes. Remember, good ventilation is essential for baking polymer clay.

The tear-away technique has many variables: rest time, temperature, copy quality, and paper type. Don't be surprised if your first efforts are less than great. Experiment with changing the variables; it might give you better results.

By the way, the piece of paper pulled from the slab has a shallow coating of polymer clay left on it. You can flatten this curled piece and bake it in the oven with the main slab and use it to create texture. The main slab is the "innie" and the paper is the "outie," so you get two textures for one; the paper has a limited life, however.

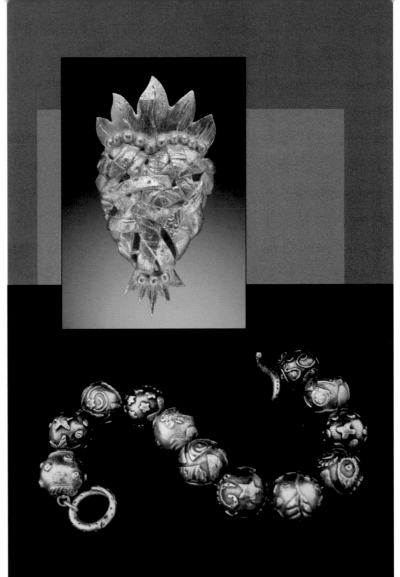

TOP
LORENA ANGULO
Milagro Heart Bead, 2007
5 x 2.6 x 1.4 cm
Metal clay, cork clay core; hand formed, stamped, stenciled
PHOTO BY DEAN POWELL

BOTTOM
BARBARA BRIGGS
Untitled, 2006
21.6 cm long
Fine silver metal clay, sterling silver, 24-karat gold
PHOTO BY ARTIST

CARVED TEXTURE PLATES

Another way of making a texture plate is to carve designs into a flat surface. I have used four materials for this: rubber eraser, linoleum, jeweler's hard carving wax, and baked polymer clay. For carving tools, use the small-scale gouges found in jewelry, model makers, art supply, and some metal clay supply catalogs. (Regular wood carving tools are usually too large for jewelry scale work.) Most art supply catalogs will have a #1 liner linoleum cutter with a handle that works very well on all of the above surfaces.

Eraser

Any type of eraser material carves easily to give you a useful texture plate or a stamp; however, most erasers are quite small. Look in the rubber stamp area of a craft store to find a soft, flexible, and easy-to-carve product about 4 x 6 x ¼ inches (10.2 x 15.2 x 0.6 cm).

Linoleum

Found in art supply catalogs and some art stores, this is the battleship gray ⅛-inch-thick (3 mm) material that some of us used in elementary school art class! If you want to make it even easier to carve, place a thin piece of cotton over the linoleum and press a dry, medium-temperature iron on it. The heat warms the material, making it carve like butter.

Jeweler's Hard Carving Wax

This relatively pricey material produces very crisp surfaces. You can buy it in precut slabs 6 x 2½ x ¼ inches (15.2 x 6.4 x 0.6 cm).

If you want a larger surface, you'll have to purchase a large block (6½ x 3⅛ x 1⅛ inches [16.5 x 8 x 2.7 cm]) and cut with a coping saw to get the size you want. Wax has the disadvantage of scratching easily if it's not stored carefully.

Baked Polymer Clay

This is my favorite surface for carving texture plates. It's reasonably priced, easy to prepare, and absolutely effortless to carve. I think any but the softest polymer clays will work, but metallic polymer clay seems to have the best texture for this use.

While baking, the slabs of polymer need to remain flat. To do this, I sandwich them between ¼-inch (6 mm) plate glass sheets (*not* window glass). Any glass or hardware store will cut a couple of pieces to your specification, making sure the edges are not sharp.

Here's how to make the slabs of baked polymer clay.

1. Condition the clay, and roll it out to about ⅛ inch (3 mm) thick. I use a pasta machine on its widest setting for the most consistent slab, but you can use a rolling pin and spacers to carefully produce a flat sheet.

2. Cut the sheet into usable pieces of any size you like. I find pieces about 4 x 5 inches (10.2 x 12.7 cm) give me a large area to carve.

3. Cover a sheet of plate glass with wax paper, arrange the polymer slabs on it, cover them with another sheet of wax paper, and top the sandwich off with the other sheet of plate glass.

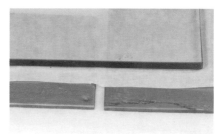

4. Place the entire assembly into a 275°F (135°C) oven for about 40 minutes. (Do not use your kitchen oven: a dedicated toaster or convection oven with good ventilation is best. The temperature can vary with the oven you use, so it's best to do a trial run.)

Do a test of the first baked sheets: after the polymer is cool, bend it; if it breaks you know you haven't baked it long enough. For the purposes of carving, however, if it's a bit under-baked, it won't matter.

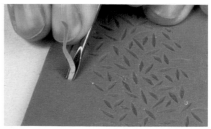

Carving a polymer clay sheet is effortless. Make sure the bits of carving detritus don't accidentally mix in with the metal clay.

LOW-TECH PHOTO ETCHING

Materials Needed

- Black-and-white image
- Photocopier (toner type)
- Printed circuit board film*
- Scissors
- Piece of copper or brass, about 20 gauge (0.813 mm)
- Steel wool
- Alcohol
- Household iron
- Thin cotton handkerchief or napkin
- Towel
- Timer/clock
- Sticky-backed shelf paper or electrical tape
- Shallow plastic container just large enough to hold the piece of metal
- Sticky wax or oil-based clay
- Tweezers
- Rubber gloves
- Copper etching solution (ferric chloride)**
- Acetone
- Paper towels

*Easy to purchase online

**Used to create circuit boards for computers, this is available at retailers of specialty electronics

Any black-and-white image, photo, drawing, or text can be etched into metal to create a texture sheet onto which you can impress or roll metal clay. This technique is a more complex procedure than any of the ones explained above, but it will give you a very permanent and crisp texture/image.

Load the special transfer film into the toner-type photocopier machine, making sure the coated side of the acetate is the side that will get printed on. Reproduce the desired image onto the film using the darkest setting on the copier—you may have to experiment. Make sure to leave at least ¾ inch (1.9 cm) of clearance on the blank film around the image.

If you prefer, you can draw your image directly on the metal, using a permanent marker or any acid-resist material. In this case, follow the instructions under Preparing the Metal, skip Applying the Image, and doodle with your marker instead, then continue to the Etching section. The marker won't be affected by the etching solution, but it will break down and may have to be renewed during a prolonged etch. This isn't technically a low-tech photo etching, but a more traditional etching procedure.

Preparing the Metal

Copper and brass seem to etch the best. The metal doesn't have to be thick; 20 gauge (0.813 mm) is ideal.

1. Mark the metal about ¾ inch (1.9 cm) larger than your image to accommodate wax supports later. Saw out the shape using a jeweler's saw, being careful to keep the sheet absolutely flat. If the metal is warped, you won't get a complete image. (You can buy precut pieces of metal that are absolutely flat.) Remove all burrs on the edges with a file.

2. Rub one side lightly with fine steel wool.

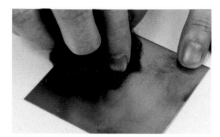

3. Clean the same side carefully with alcohol to remove any grease from the surface. From now on, don't handle the cleaned front of your metal; hold it only by the edges.

Applying the Image

Set the iron for cotton/linen, 265 to 295°F (129.4 to 146.1°C). Keep the setting on dry and do *not* fill the appliance with water for steam.

1. Cover your worktable with a towel. Set the clean side of the metal facing up on the towel and place the film with the toner/image side of the film touching the metal.

2. Lay a thin cloth over the metal and place the iron on top for 5 minutes. Don't move the iron, or you'll blur the image.

3. Allow the metal to cool completely. Peel off the film slowly from one corner, checking that the entire image has transferred. If it hasn't, carefully replace the film and press with the iron for another 2 minutes. Cool again and peel off the film completely. The black toner is now securely adhered to the metal.

Etching

The back and edges of the metal plate need to be protected from the copper etching solution (CES) or ferric chloride. To shield the metal, you can brush it with lacquer or nail polish, cover it with electrical tape or sticky-backed shelf paper, or paint it with any acid resist. The sticky-backed shelf paper seems to be the easiest to use.

1. Build little wax feet or supports on the corners to hold the plate off the surface of the container holding the CES. The surface to be etched should face down.

2. Select a shallow plastic container just large enough to accommodate your piece of metal and pour in enough CES to cover the piece.

3. Check the plate every 15 minutes, using tweezers to handle it. The length of time in the CES varies according to how deep of an etch you desire. Etching too deeply will cause the metal clay to catch, and you won't get a clean impression. Usually 20 to 30 minutes of etching gives a good depth. You can paint on nail polish /lacquer to stop out selected areas if you want to vary the depth of the etch.

4. When you reach the desired depth of etch, wear rubber gloves to wash off the CES with water.

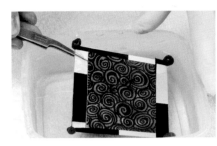

5. Remove the black resist with acetone.

Store the used CES in an old plastic bottle to use again (you'll notice it doesn't etch quite as fast as the new chemical does). To dispose of old CES, contact your local hazardous waste authority.

TOP

DONNA LEWIS
Fun Beads, 2007
Tallest, 6 x 2.1 x 1.5 cm
Metal clay, fresh water pearls; coreless constructed
PHOTO BY ARTIST

BOTTOM

PATRICIA CARLSON
Glacial Pools, 2006
3 x 3 x 41 cm
Metal clay, lab created gems; mold created
PHOTO BY LARRY SANDERS

PHOTOPOLYMER PLATES

This method of creating texture plates is surprisingly simple and relatively inexpensive. It's used by the letterpress printing industry and by artist/printmakers.

To make a photopolymer plate (PPP), you'll create a black-and-white image similar to one you would use for the low-tech photo etch, then transfer this image to transparent film—acetate or overhead projector film. Finally, you'll overlay the film onto the light-sensitive polymer surface of the PPP and expose it to UV light. The areas struck by the UV light will harden and cure the polymer, while those masked by the black of the design will remain water soluble and can be gently scrubbed away under water. What results is an exact etching of the original drawing, photograph, pattern, or text.

Creating the Transparency

You can convert any image or design to black and white by using a copy machine or a graphics program on a computer. Your local office supply store undoubtedly has an expert in the copy department who can do all this work for you, if necessary, and then transfer your image to acetate or overhead projector film. What's most important is to reproduce the image in the darkest black possible. If any light can penetrate the black areas of your image, the exposure part of the process won't work. I've used an opaque, permanent black marker or a marker that dispenses paint to color in areas of the black toner that seem to be less than dense. This appears to be another good solution for completely darkening the acetate sheet.

I've tried the printer attached to my desktop computer and it doesn't print sufficiently black. A successful alternative is to print two images and piggyback one exactly on top of the other to give maximum black. If you do use your ink-jet printer, be sure to choose the correct paper setting. I set my printer for glossy paper when I run overhead projector film in the machine.

Cutting the PPP

Several companies sell sheets of PPP, which is light sensitive and comes packaged in a heavy, black plastic bag. It's important to prevent its exposure to any light source, so when you're ready to use it, only unpack what you need, cut it up without delay, and return the rest to the black bag immediately.

PPP has a thin plastic or steel backing. The plastic is easy to cut by scoring and it stays flat during curing. However, the sheets tend to curl with time and that makes it challenging to roll a sheet of metal clay onto the PPP. The metal-backed PPP stays flat but needs to be cut with a jeweler's saw. Using tin snips or a similar shearlike tool requires careful cutting to avoid warping the PPP; be careful of the sharp edges.

When you cut a piece of PPP, make the overall dimensions about ¾ inch (1.9 cm) larger than the image. This allows room for the clamps on the frame and for your spacers when rolling metal clay onto the design.

1. To cut plastic-backed plate, place the polymer side up. The polymer is protected with a thin sheet of plastic that stays on until the frame is set up. Use a marker on this protective cover to delineate where you need to cut.

2. Use a metal straight edge and a utility knife to make several strokes, scoring down through the polymer until you begin to cut into the backing. A few cuts into the plastic layer suffice.

3. Bend the PPP back and forth until it snaps apart. If you're not ready to set up the frame, place the PPP in the black plastic bag until that time.

I use PPP that's 8½ x 11½ inches (21.6 x 29.2 cm), and 0.06 inch (1.5 mm) thick. This size cuts up easily into useful plates, and the thickness gives ample depth for the etch. The thicker PPPs make it possible to use masks and double exposures to create variations of depth. PPPs are also available in a shallower depth (0.037 inch [0.9 mm] thick), which is useful when only a subtle amount of relief is desired. For instance, when using the technique of kum boo, a high relief will make complete burnishing of the gold foil very difficult.

Light Sources

As a light source, I use an 18-inch (45.7 cm) 15-watt black lightbulb purchased from a home improvement store, along with a light fixture meant to be screwed under a kitchen cabinet to light the countertop. I've set up my light fixture on blocks of wood to get the correct distance from bulb to frame. Warm up the black light by turning it on for about 15 seconds before placing your frame underneath.

An alternative setup is a device that uses UV light to cure acrylic fingernails, sold at housewares and beauty-supply stores. Set up the UV light source so it's 2 to 3 inches (5.1 to 7.6 cm) from the surface of the frame.

You can certainly use sunlight, but then it's essential to make a test strip, because where you live, the intensity of the sun, and the time of day will all be factors in exposure time. For instance, exposure at midday in sunny Key West, Florida, will be different than on a partly cloudy day in Chicago, Illinois. Just to give you an idea, in Hawaii on a sunny day, exposure time is 1 minute, 5 seconds.

No matter which light source you plan to use, if you're setting up a PPP system for the first time, here's how to make a test strip for it.

1. Cut a 1 x 5-inch (2.5 x 12.7 cm) piece of PPP and place an image of the same dimension on it. Cover all but 1 inch (2.5 cm) of this plate with cardboard, and expose it to the light source for 20 seconds.

2. Move the cardboard to uncover the next 1 inch (2.5 cm) of PPP, and expose it for another 20 seconds.

3. Proceed this way three more times until the whole PPP is uncovered.

By a sequence of exposures, you'll have an idea of how much time is required for a certain depth with your particular light source. Select the section you like best, and use that exposure time.

The Contact Frame

The frame allows the image to rest on the polymer surface with enough pressure to prevent any UV light from seeping under the black areas of the design. This tight fit results in crisp lines.

The frame consists of two pieces of glass (I got two cheap 5 x 7-inch [12.7 x 17.8 cm] picture frames, which I dismantled; watch the sharp edges!); one piece of bubble wrap, cut to 5 x 7 inches (12.7 x 17.8 cm), to help achieve an even, tight fit; and four 3-inch-wide (7.6 cm) bulldog clips, obtained from an office supply store.

1. To assemble the PPP in the frame, begin by placing one piece of glass on the worktable. Lay the bubble wrap sheet on top of the glass.

2. Next, place the PPP, backing side down, on the glass. Remove the protective plastic from the polymer side.

3. With the printed side down and in direct contact with the polymer surface, place your film or image in the center of the PPP. Place the other piece of glass, clean and fingerprint free, on top of the PPP and image.

4. Secure all four sides and all five layers with the bulldog clips, making sure the clips don't obscure the image.

Exposure

Set the frame under the warmed-up black light, 2 to 3 inches (5.1 to 7.6 cm) away, and expose the PPP for 1 minute and 30 seconds, or expose for half that time if your design consists mostly of fine lines. These exposure times give a generous depth to the PPP; lesser times result in a more shallow relief.

Developing/Rinsing

After exposing the PPP for the proper amount of time, turn off your light and remove the PPP from the frame. Use a soft brush, such as a baby's hairbrush, a soft natural bristle brush, or a mushroom brush, to rinse it in a tub of tepid water. Don't scrub too hard, or some of the polymer might separate from the backing. This procedure should take only a few minutes.

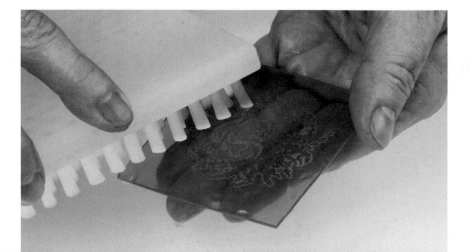

The PPP will feel sticky. Use a lint-free cloth or a chamois to pat away excess water. Dry it further with a hair dryer set on low. Any water present on the surface of the PPP will affect the next curing process.

Final Curing

Place the PPP—no contact frame needed—under the UV light and reexpose it for 3 minutes to completely harden and cure the polymer. After final curing, keep all surfaces lightly oiled with a bit of vegetable or olive oil to preserve the PPP.

To store the plates, lightly oil and wrap each in tissue paper and seal them in a plastic bag. Open air will deteriorate the polymer. If you're storing a stack of PPPs, insert a sheet of cardboard between each. Keep your plates in a cool, dry place.

RIGHT

WENDY WALLIN MALINOW
Spiked Pods, 2007
Largest bead, 2.5 x 2.5 x
2.5 cm
Metal clay, polymer clay,
linen, patina; hollow formed,
textured
PHOTO BY COURTNEY FRISSE

LEFT

DORIS WAGNER
Untitled, 2007
44.5 cm long
Silver metal clay, lava rock beads,
PMC3, fine silver beads; hollow
formed, polished
PHOTO BY MARGOT GEIST

TIPS FOR USING TEXTURE PLATES

When you make a texture plate, try to leave a plain border all the way around the textured area. Your spacers will rest on this surface. We don't always have the luxury of planning for this, so be aware that if you're using spacers to create a consistent sheet of textured clay, the spacers will take up some of the space of the texture plate.

If I have a small texture plate and I want to use all of it, I flank the plate with material that exactly matches the thickness of the plate onto which I can place my spacers. This way, I can utilize all of the texture plate.

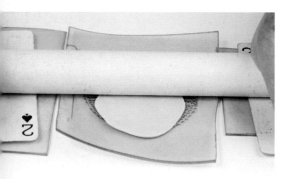

Release Agents

All texture plates except those made of two-part silicone mold material require the application of some kind of release agent. I have a paintbrush dedicated to use with only liquid olive oil or solid olive oil balm. Lightly load the brush with oil and scrub it in all directions on the texture plate. Don't overload it with oil. It's also helpful to apply a light film of oil to the surface of the sheet of metal clay you plan to texture.

I prefer to use talcum powder or cornstarch on rubber stamp texture plates because, over time, the olive oil seems to harden the rubber. A pouncer is ideal for applying a light, even coat to the texture plate. To make your own, refer to page 000.

Use the pouncer to shake a small amount of powder onto the texture plate. (Wear a dust mask while pouncing.) If I use the powder on the texture plate, I use it on the metal clay sheet as well; oil and powder combine to make an unwelcome, gooey mixture!

Impressing Metal Clay onto Texture Plates

1. To prepare metal clay for use on a texture plate, roll out a slab of it to a thickness one card more than what you want the finished thickness to be. For instance, for most bead construction I like to use a two-card-thick piece of clay, so I begin by rolling out a piece three cards thick.

2. Cut the sheet of clay to fit the dimension of just the textured area of the texture plate. If the metal clay covers the entire texture plate, you'll have no room to place spacers on the untextured borders of the plate.

3. Apply release agent to the texture plate and to the metal clay sheet.

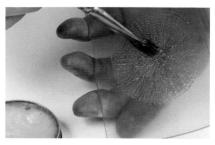

4. Position the spacers on the texture plate and lay the metal clay sheet over the textured area.

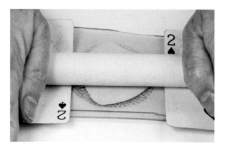

5. Roll carefully with consistent pressure from the midpoint to each end to get a good impression.

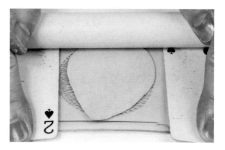

6. Gently flip up a corner of the metal clay and judge the quality of the texture. If it isn't deep enough, place the corner back down without changing the position of the clay and reroll it.

Text

If your image contains text, be sure to place it backward on the texture plate, or it won't read correctly when you peel off the metal clay after rolling it onto the plate. To get your text backward, you can rely on computer graphics programs that you operate yourself or ask the printing expert at the office supply store to reverse your original artwork before transferring it to the transparent film used for low-tech photo etching or PPPs.

When forming wet, textured clay into a curved mold, don't press too hard; you'll mess up the texture.

Drying Techniques

Once your metal clay has texture, you're ready to dry it in the desired form. For instance, if you wanted a lentil bead, you would cut out a circle and drape the metal clay over a form, such as a lightbulb, and let it dry to that domed shape.

At times, such as in the formation of box beads, we need to dry the clay absolutely flat. I like to let the metal clay dry naturally to prevent warping, which will make it difficult to construct the box.

1. Take a piece of facial tissue and peel the two layers apart. Set one ply on a flat surface and place your wet metal clay on it, making sure the paper has no wrinkles in it.

2. Allow the metal clay to air-dry, checking it within the first 15 to 20 minutes, and gently pat down any warps that may be developing.

3. When the surface of the clay begins to harden, carefully flip it over to allow the untextured side to dry. Monitor the drying from time to time and you will have a perfectly flat piece of textured metal clay.

BARBARA BECKER SIMON
Study in Gray & White II, 2003
2.5 x 53 cm
Fine silver, glass beads, sterling silver, freshwater pearl; beads created around combustible core
PHOTO BY LARRY SANDERS

THE PROJECTS

Before diving into the projects, you need to know about the eagle eye. This is what I call a detailed, critical inspection of all surfaces and seams of the project, and it should happen just before placing the metal clay in the kiln. Turn the bead over and over in your hands and look at every aspect to make sure you've achieved the highest level of craftsmanship.

Look for such things as:

- Stray slip

- Coarse emery scratches or tool marks of any kind that aren't intentional textural elements

- Burs of clay left from cutting tools

- Holes, cracks, and poorly attached seams

- Poorly disguised seams

- Thin or weak areas that need more strength, such as bail connections, etc.

Now's the time to notice and repair these flaws, because once you fire the piece, they're not easily remedied.

Now that I've given you the background information, you're ready to begin making beads. The 22 projects in this book all consist of singular forms—just a box, for instance, or only a sphere or a wedge. Once you know what you're doing, I encourage you to take it a step further by combining two or more forms to create a bead. For example, you could make a lentil and attach a polygon to it. Or make a sphere and attach lobes to it, similar to those on the Porcupine Bead (opposite page). Don't be shy about concocting complex forms and combining the techniques shown in the projects. Okay, it's time to start. Have fun!

BIAS-WRAPPED BEAD

Get more mileage from a texture plate: after wrapping a narrow strip of textured clay around a straw on the diagonal, it's easy to transform the texture. Fill in and otherwise disguise the seams, which butt up flush against one another, to create yet another level of visual interest.

MATERIALS

Metal clay
Slip
Liver of sulfur

TOOLS

Basic Tool Kit (page 12)
Texture plate of your choice

STEP BY STEP

1. Prepare a 3½ x ½ inch (8.9 x 1.3 cm) sheet of textured metal clay. Lightly oil a drinking straw and wrap the metal clay strip in a diagonal direction around the straw. Carefully butt the seams against one another without compromising the texture.

2. Use a blade to cut off the pointy ends, creating a 1-inch-long (2.5 cm) cylinder. Let dry. Caulk clay into the seam, being sure not to cover up the texture on either side of the seam; allow it to dry.

3. Remove the cylinder from the straw. Caulk clay into the interior of the seam, reaching in as far as possible. Let dry. Groom the outer seam of the bead. It may be necessary to "reproduce" or continue the texture over the seams; use your judgment.

4. With an emery board, shape the ends of the bead so they're a clean 90° angle to the shaft of the cylinder.

5. To make the end caps, roll a metal clay sheet that is three cards thick. (This may be a textured sheet.) Cut two circles from the sheet and let them dry. Sand the edges of the circles to a scratch-free finish with an emery board. Use a needle tool to pierce the exact center of each circle. Twirl a craft knife in each pierced mark until you have an opening a bit smaller than the inner diameter of the bead.

6. Using a generous amount of slip, attach the end caps to the cylinder, centering the holes. Let dry. Clean the holes by scraping away any excess clay and slip, caulking in clay where needed.

(continued on next page)

NICOLE BSULLAK
Abundance, 2007
· 7.6 x 3.8 cm
Clay, metal clay, silver; encaustic
PHOTO BY ARTIST

7. Using the tip of a craft knife, remove any excess slip from the seam where the end cap meets outside of the cylinder. Caulk and let dry. Give your bead a visual once-over, and then fire it supported by vermiculite or a fiber blanket. Finish it with a patina using liver of sulfur and steel wool.

Variations

• Make the bead without end caps.

• Spread out the wrapping, leaving space between the seam areas. **Note:** Make sure that there is some sort of end cap securely connected to the open spiral shape or it will be weak.

• Use larger straws.

• Make the width of the strip narrower or wider.

• Cut out the strip with decorative edges and use those as a design element.

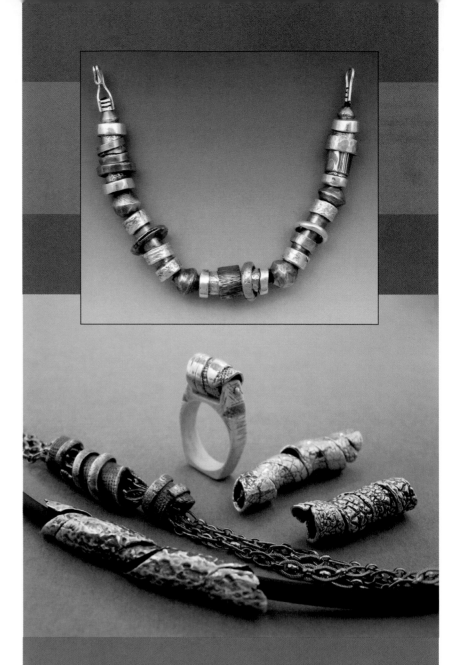

TOP
HADAR JACOBSON
Spinning Beads, 2007
19.1 cm long
Metal clay, copper, brass, bronze, mokume gane; fired, soldered, etched, hammered
PHOTO BY ARTIST

BOTTOM
DONNA LEWIS
Tubes, 2007
Tallest, 5.5 x 0.8 cm
Metal clay; rolled, attached, patterned
PHOTO BY ARTIST

EMBELLISHED
BIAS-WRAPPED BEAD

Add dimension and texture to this bead by overlapping the seams as you wrap the metal clay strip and, later in the process, by carving the dried clay. The stones set on either end add a dash of color, and the vertical orientation of the bead makes it truly unique.

MATERIALS

Metal clay
2 fire-friendly, 6-mm stones,
   cabochon or faceted
Slip

TOOLS

Basic Tool Kit (page 12)
V-shaped gouge or carving tool

STEP BY STEP

1. Roll out a three-card-thick strip of metal clay that measures 5 x ½ inches (12.7 x 1.3 cm). With a straight edge, refine the sheet's width to ⅜ inch (1 cm).

2. Lightly oil a drinking straw. Wrap the metal clay strip around the straw on the diagonal, overlapping each new turn ¹⁄₁₆ inch (1.6 mm) on top of the previous wrap to form a stepped cylinder. Cut off the pointy ends to form a cylinder that is approximately 1 inch (2.5 cm) long. When dry, slip the cylinder off the straw. Caulk the interior seams to make them strong, reaching inside as best you can. Set aside to let dry.

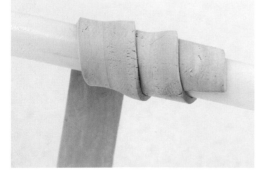

3. Using a V-shaped gouge or carving tool, make parallel cuts on the surface of the cylinder to give it a "fluted" appearance. When the cuts are complete, make sure the top of each "flute" shape is smoothly rounded. Using the emery board, file the ends of the cylinder to square them off to a 90° angle.

4. With your fingers, roll a little sphere of metal clay about ⅜ inch (1 cm) in diameter. Gently mash the sphere down into a patty shape that is ⅛ inch (3 mm) tall. With a beverage straw, pierce a hole in the middle (photo 6) of the patty. Repeat this step to form a second metal clay patty.

5. Gently press a 6-mm stone into one soft patty until the top of the stone is slightly below the top surface of the metal clay. Repeat for the second stone and patty. Let both stone settings dry.

6. Clean any dry clay off the front and the back of the stones. Use slip to glue one setting to each end of the cylinder. Let dry. Clean any oozed slip from the seams at the ends of the bead.

7. This bead hangs vertically. Determine which end will be the top of the bead. On opposite sides of the bead, measure ¼ inch (6 mm) down from the top. Twirl a craft knife or a drill bit to cut a hole at each of these locations. Clean any ragged edges on the holes and give your bead the eagle eye. Fire it supported on vermiculite or a fiber blanket. Finish as desired.

CAPPED
CYLINDER BEAD

This bead just begs to be touched. Despite its simplicity, it packs a lot of punch and covers a whole range of techniques, including lap seaming, mitering, and blending texture across a seam and from one plane to another.

MATERIALS

Metal clay, lump and
     syringe forms
Slip

TOOLS

Basic Tool Kit (page 12)
Cylindrical form
     (such as a marker,
     large straw, or dowel)
Cellophane tape
Texture plate of your choice

STEP BY STEP

1. To make a paper template, wrap a piece of paper around the cylindrical form and mark the length. Add ¾ inch (1.7 cm) to this length. Cut the paper to the desired width for the finished bead. Set the paper template aside.

Note: Making the metal clay strip the exact circumference of the cylinder can stretch and thin the metal clay, causing a weak lap seam. It is good practice to make a template larger than needed, because it is always easier to cut away excess metal clay than to try to create or add more material.

2. Lightly oil the cylindrical form and tightly wrap it with one layer of plastic wrap. Secure the edges of the plastic wrap with tape. (Don't tape the plastic wrap directly to the cylindrical form, or it will be difficult to remove later.) Make sure that about 1½ inches (3.8 cm) of plastic wrap

sticks out past the ends of the bead. This will be a plastic "handle" you can use to pull the bead off the cylindrical form when it is almost dry. Set the form aside.

3. Apply a release agent to the texture plate. Roll out a textured sheet of metal clay that is two cards thick. Use the template as a guide to shape the sheet.

4. Wrap the textured metal clay sheet around the cylindrical form, leaving the plastic handle exposed. Because the clay strip is longer than needed, its ends will overlap to make a lap seam. As illustrated in the diagrams, the lap seam affords more surface area for slip than the butt seam does, and it therefore makes a stronger seam.

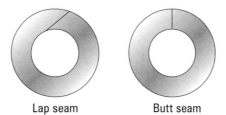

Lap seam   Butt seam

5. To make a lap seam, use a razor blade to cut through both layers of the overlapped metal clay at a 45°angle. Remove the excess clay and secure the seam with slip, gently pressing the seam flat without mashing the texture. Use a good

amount of slip; the excess will be easy to clean off later. Let this sit to dry until the surface of the clay is a bit stiff.

Note: If you let the metal clay cylinder dry on the form completely, it will shrink a bit and may cause the seam to pull apart. Let the clay dry only partially, so it can be carefully pulled off without losing its shape. The rest of the drying will be completed off the form so the seam stays intact.

6. When the cylinder is partially dry, cut the plastic wrap close to the edge of the clay with a razor or craft knife. Slowly and carefully pull the plastic wrap handle until the metal clay comes off the form. Being a little

stiff, the clay cylinder will easily *set on its edge* and complete the drying process. At this stage, you can gently pry the plastic wrap from the inside of the form or let it remain in place until the cylinder is dry.

7. While the cylinder is drying, prepare the metal clay sheet for the end caps. Cut out two circles for the end caps, each 40 to 50 percent larger than the diameter of the cylinder. For example, if the outer diameter of the cylinder is ³⁄₄ inch (1.9 cm), cut the circles 1¹⁄₈ inches (2.8 cm) in diameter. This way, you will have excess clay to trim to the exact size and shape. Set the end caps aside to dry.

8. Handling the dry clay cylinder with care, secure the inside seam by caulking it with clay. On the outside of the seam, flick off any oozed slip and caulk any gaps. Take a close look at the way the texture pattern is arranged at the seam. Disguise the location of the seam either by adding more clay or by carving clay away. Let the clay dry.

9. Using an emery board or emery paper on a flat tabletop, file the ends of the cylinder at 90° angles to the sides. To miter the ends, use a craft knife to carefully carve away the *inside* of both ends until they have a knife-edge. This can also be done with a half-round needle file or similar small, half-round abrasive stick.

10. To avoid confusion later, use a pencil to mark one of the dry end caps with the letter A. Make the mark in the center of the nontextured side. Choose one end of the cylinder and mark an A on the inside. These marks will help with registration and help you remember which end is which.

11. Place end cap A texture-side down on the table. Center end A of the cylinder on top of the end cap. While holding on to the cylinder, take a very sharp pencil and outline the cylinder on the end cap. Before separating the two parts, make a register mark on the end cap and a matching one on the outside of the cylinder. This will help identify placement as you fit the end cap to the cylinder.

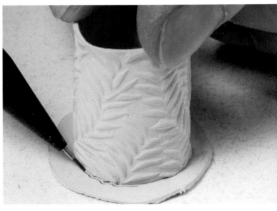

12. Following the pencil line, carefully trim away the excess from circle A. Take a craft knife or emery board and miter the edge of the circle to a 45° knife-edge. Don't cut away any of the end cap's circumference.

(continued on next page)

13. Place the register marks for the A parts together and see how closely they fit. There should be no space between the end of the cylinder and the end cap. If you see space, take the craft knife and trim away the excess until the end cap drops into place and fits flush into the cylinder.

14. Line up the registration marks on the A parts, and then glue them together with a generous amount of slip. Let dry.

15. Repeat steps 11 through 14 for the other end of the cylinder and the second end cap.

16. When all seams are dry, flick off the oozed slip and determine where any caulking needs to be done. Using a craft knife, carving tool, emery board, or any combination of these tools, groom the edges of the seams so that the texture design flows from the end cap to the cylinder.

17. Make a centered hole in each end cap and clean up any ragged edges. If desired, add a little collar around the edge of the hole using syringe or a rolled worm of clay. Give the bead the eagle eye and fire it supported with vermiculite or a fiber blanket. Finish as desired.

Variations

- Dome the end caps.

- Try concave end caps instead of flat ones.

- File the ends of the cylinder at angles.

- File the ends of the cylinder to points and cap with four flat pieces—two on each end.

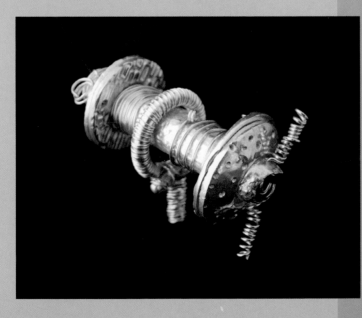

SIMPLE SPHERE

Make a classic round bead more interesting by adding a layer of appliquéd metal clay to parts of it. You can texture the appliquéd layer with any design that appeals to you—the possibilities are endless.

MATERIALS

Metal clay
Styrofoam ball, ⅞ inch (2.2 cm)
   in diameter, coated with thin
   layer of wax or white glue
Slip

TOOLS

Basic Tool Kit (page 12)
Old toothbrush, coarse emery
   paper, or other textured material
   (optional)
Toothpick
Texture plate of your choice

Note: Because the spherical form is inherently strong, it is possible to make fairly large beads. Even the higher firing clay can be used for a sphere as large as 1¼ inches (3.2 cm) in diameter without inner support. See the Complex Core Bead project on page 132 for more information on internal supports.

STEP BY STEP

1. Roll out a sheet of metal clay that is two cards thick. Cut out two circles, each with a 1-inch (2.5 cm) diameter. Cover the remaining clay with plastic wrap and set aside.

2. Use the palm of your hand to mold one clay circle around a section of the Styrofoam ball.

Mold the second clay circle on the opposite side of the ball. You will have an empty strip between the edges of the molded clay.

3. Moisten the edges of the molded clay with water. Patch the empty strip using the leftover pieces of clay sheet from step 1. Make sure the edges overlap. Use the rubber-tipped tool to mash and blend the seams, creating a strong seam and a smooth surface.

Note: When fired, seams that are not fully blended will be noticeable and may even separate.

4. While the clay is still soft, you can apply a light, subtle texture on the base layer of the bead. Try pressing an old toothbrush or some coarse emery paper onto the surface, or leave the surface smooth if you prefer.

5. Use a needle tool to pierce two holes in the bead, and enlarge them to accommodate your hanging material. Insert a toothpick in one of the holes to act as a handle. Set the bead aside.

6. Prepare a textured metal clay sheet rolled to three cards thick. Use a craft knife to cut out a small simple shape, such as a triangle. Separate the shape from the sheet. Cover the remaining metal clay with plastic wrap to keep it moist.

7. Use slip to glue the simple shape to the bead. Gently push the textured shape to conform to the curves of the bead. Continue to cut and add simple textured shapes to the bead until it is covered, taking care not to cover the holes.

8. Give the bead the eagle eye. Place it on a support material and fire. Finish as desired.

LEFT
BARBARA BECKER SIMON
Peaches in Regalia, 2000
3 x 52 cm
Fine silver, glass beads,
sterling silver, freshwater
pearls, metal clay beads;
lampworked; hollow over
complex core
PHOTO BY LARRY SANDERS

RIGHT
ANNE LINGENER-REECE
Balls of Leaves, 2003
18 x 18 x 2.5 cm
Fine silver mesh, metal clay, fine
silver sheet, lava beads, coral
branches, fine silver wire, black
antique enamel; formed, air dried,
embellished, kiln fired, polished,
enameled, cut, hand formed
PHOTOS BY ARTIST

MIRROR-IMAGE
BEADS

Drying wet clay over a form will give you one side of these beads. By making a duplicate, or twin, and connecting them edge to edge, you create a hollow form.

These next projects are variations of this concept.

LENTIL BEAD
WITH GEMSTONES

Sparkling gemstones serve as the focal points for organic textures. You have many options for the form over which to dry this reversible bead, including lightbulbs, plastic Easter eggs, ping-pong balls, and marbles. Each form creates a different curve, resulting in different profiles, high or low.

MATERIALS

Metal clay
Slip
2 fire-friendly gemstones

TOOLS

Basic Tool Kit (page 12)
Curved drying form of your choice
2 texture plates of your choice
Emery paper, 180 or 200 grit

STEP BY STEP

1. Lightly oil the curved drying form. Roll out one sheet of clay for each of the two texture plates. Cut out one 1-inch (2.5 cm) circle from each of the textured metal clay sheets. Place both textured circles on the drying form, making sure they are centered. Gently coax the clay to conform to the curve without mashing its texture. Let it dry.

2. Place one dry clay dome on the emery paper, edge-side down. Gently sweep the dome back and forth, until it's flush with the tabletop. Repeat with the second dome.

3. Hold the two domes edge to edge. If the circles don't match exactly, determine which is larger. Place that one back on the emery paper and sand it until it matches its mate. Use a generous amount of slip and gently press the edges of the two domes together. Allow the bead to dry.

4. Use a craft knife and/or a carving tool to blend the texture of the two sides of the bead at the seam. Caulk any holes or cracks.

5. Move a slightly damp paintbrush back and forth over the seam to groom the edges. Work carefully—too much water on the clay will blur the crispness of your texture.

6. Determine where you want to set the gemstones, one on each side of the lentil bead. Use a drill, a stone-setting bur, or the tip of a craft knife to cut a hole into the clay surface at these points. Enlarge and miter the holes so that the girdles of the stones are flush with the surface of the metal clay.

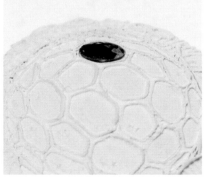

7. Place one gemstone in one hole. Use a syringe to pipe a collar of metal clay around the stone. Make sure the collar overlaps the girdle of the stone

ever so slightly and that the ends of the collar slightly overlap as well. Check the connection of the syringed clay. Make sure there are no gaps and that the seam is disguised.

8. Use a syringe to set the second gemstone on the other side of the bead. This time, however, pipe tiny beads of clay to create mock prongs. The prongs should come over the top of the stone enough to secure it, but shouldn't cover too much of its surface. Make sure the connection of the syringe metal clay (prongs) to the base metal clay (lentil bead) is strong. Once dry, check the connection again, caulking small bits of clay, if necessary.

(continued on next page)

Lentil Bead with Gemstones   79

9. Consider where you want to place the holes in the bead. In the bead shown, the holes are placed at 10 o'clock and 2 o'clock from the top of the bead. Use a craft knife to gently carve away the edge of the bead until the opening is large enough to accommodate your hanging device. If you need the holes to be round, use a drill bit at this point.

10. Pipe a collar of syringe metal clay around the holes to give them a finished look. Once dry, make sure the syringed metal clay around the holes is secure; caulk if needed. Give your lentil bead the eagle eye. Place it on support material and fire. Finish as desired.

Variations

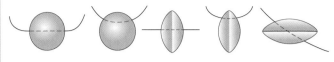

- Try placing the holes in different locations.

- Pierce the clay for an open look.
- Create the domes with worms or syringe clay instead of sheet clay.
- Make a band ring to connect the two domes.

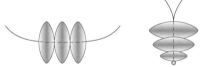

- Truncate the lentil shape and cap with a flat sheet.

- Line up several lentil beads and use slip to permanently connect them.

- Use different curvatures for the two domes.
- Make one lentil bead, cut it in half, and cap the ends.

PAM WITTFELD
Hollow Bead Bracelet, 2005
Largest bead, 1.8 x 1 cm
PMC3, sterling silver
spacers, sterling silver wire,
patina; draped
PHOTO BY ARTIST

PILLOW BEAD

This variation of the lentil bead features an angular form instead of a circular shape. For extra visual interest, use the easiest of tricks: simply press the front and the back sides with different textures.

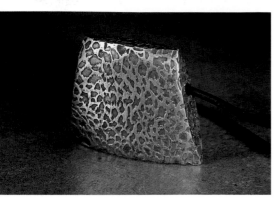

MATERIALS

Metal clay
Slip

TOOLS

Basic Tool Kit (page 12)
Dome-shaped drying forms, such
    as Easter eggs or lightbulbs
2 different texture plates

STEP BY STEP

1. Determine a trapezoid shape for your bead and make a paper pattern of that shape. For the trapezoid shown, the top edge is 1⁵⁄16 inches (3.3 cm), the bottom edge is 1¹¹⁄16 inches (4.3 cm), and the bead is 1⁵⁄16 inches (3.4 cm) tall. The angles at the bottom corners are each 80°.

2. Oil the dome forms. Create two sheets of two-card-thick metal clay, one from each of the texture plates. Lay the paper pattern on the clay and cut out one trapezoid from each textured sheet. Center the trapezoids over the apex of the domes (the clay should conform to the curve of the dome) and let dry.

3. Choose one texture for the sides of the bead and make a two-card-thick metal clay sheet for the four sides of the bead. Set aside to dry.

4. Align the two trapezoids at their matching corners, use a little slip to tack the corners together, and let dry. Handling the dry form with care, caulk a generous amount of clay inside each corner. These points of contact must be very strong. Let the trapezoid and the new textured sheet (step 3) dry completely.

5. Use a coarse emery board to file each open side of the trapezoid until each is even and flush with the file. Look at the form and double-check the symmetry of the shape.

6. Place one open side of the trapezoid down on the wrong side of the textured metal clay sheet. Using a very sharp pencil, outline the form on the sheet. Make registration marks so you can always place the flat piece in the same position. Use a craft knife or similar tool to cut out the outlined shape.

7. Use a craft knife to miter the flat piece to a knife-edge. Miter the corresponding opening of the trapezoid in a similar fashion. Fit the two corresponding pieces together and make any adjustments needed so that the flat piece drops down into it and is flush with, the opening in the trapezoid. Don't worry if there are small gaps or slits; these will be caulked later. Once the fit pleases you, use a generous amount of slip to glue the two pieces together. Let dry. Caulk a bit of clay onto the inside of the seam for strength and let it dry.

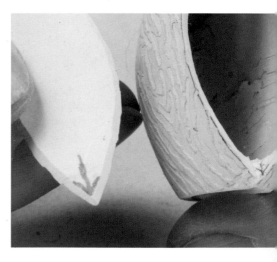

8. Repeat steps 6 and 7 three times to create flat pieces and close the remaining sides of the bead. After the form is dry, inspect each seam and flick off any dry slip that has oozed out. Look for gaps and caulk clay into them.

9. "Reconcile" the textures on either side of the seams by carving away clay with a craft knife and/or a carving tool or by adding a little clay. The object is to make the two sides of the seam flow into one another. After grooming all seams, use a damp paintbrush to soften any tool marks.

10. Determine locations for two holes in the bead and use a craft knife or drill bit to make the holes. Give the bead a final eagle eye. Place the bead on support material and fire it. Finish as desired.

Variations

- Create a pillow bead with open sides.

- Create variations on outside shapes.

TOP
LORA HART
Untitled, 2006
5.7 x 2.4 x 2.2 cm
Metal clay, silk, pearls; hand formed, fabricated, oxidized
PHOTO BY MARSHA THOMAS

BOTTOM
TERRY KOVALCIK
Botanicals, 2006
2.5 x 2.5 x 1 cm
Fine silver clay, silver sheet clay; hollow formed
PHOTO BY CORRIN JACOBSEN KOVALCIK

PEBBLE BEAD

This bead arrives at its pleasing feel and shape naturally.
You'll take a mold of a smooth, rounded pebble, so select a
polished river rock without undercuts or sharp angles. Later,
this allows the metal clay to come out of the mold easily,
without losing any thickness.

MATERIALS

Two-part silicone mold material
River stone or pebble
Metal clay
Slip

TOOLS

Basic Tool Kit (page 12)
Emery paper, 180 or 220 grit

STEP BY STEP

1. Following the manufacturer's instructions, mix a batch of two-part silicone mold material until a solid color is achieved. Form the mold material into a patty shape that's not too flat. (The patty should be thicker than half the height of your stone.) Press the stone halfway into the mold. Let the mold sit and cure with the stone in place.

2. Mix a second batch of the mold material. Press it around the exposed side of the stone and down to meet the previously cured silicone material. Let this cure.

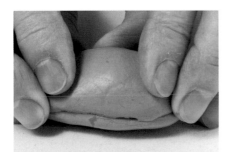

3. Once the mold has hardened, use a little bit of force to pull the two sides apart. Set the stone aside.

4. Choose one side of the mold to work with. Roll out a sheet of metal clay that's two cards thick. Cut out a piece of this sheet that is a bit larger than the shape of the mold opening.

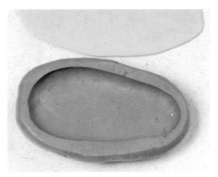

5. Press the clay into the mold with your fingertips. Be careful not to stretch or rip the clay as you coax it to conform to the mold. If the mold is deep, watch for crinkles and folds in the sheet. Trim off any excess clay to help prevent crimping. Set this aside to dry.

6. Repeat steps 4 and 5 for the second side of the mold.

7. Pop the two pieces of dried clay out of the molds. Trim off any excess clay with a craft knife. One at a time, sweep each metal clay form back and forth across the emery paper to even out the edges. Don't take off more clay than is necessary or the curve at the sides of pebble won't look right. Repeat until both sides fit together.

8. Use a generous amount of thick slip to attach the two sides of the bead. When the slip has dried, groom the seam by eliminating excess slip and caulking any gaps, taking care to disguise the seam.

9. Determine where you want to make two holes in the bead. Drill and clean the holes. Place the bead on support material and fire it. Finish as desired.

DONUT BEAD

The hole in the middle of this bead—hence the name—makes

it unique. It's formed over an armature of polymer clay. I like

to string the finished bead by looping a cord through the hole,

although you could take another approach by piercing the bead in

the spots where you'd traditionally place bead holes.

MATERIALS

Polymer clay
Talcum powder
Metal clay
Slip

TOOLS

Basic Tool Kit (page 12)
Wax paper
Dome form, such as a ping-pong
    ball or 25-watt A15 lightbulb,
    1⅛ inches (4.7 cm) in diameter
Circular cookie cutter, ⅝ inch
    (1.6 cm) in diameter
Cookie sheet
Oven
Emery papers, 180 and 220 grit
Texture plate of your choice

STEP BY STEP

1. To make the mold, roll a ball of polymer clay between your hands into a sphere that is about 1 inch (2.5 cm) in diameter. Place the sphere on the wax paper and slowly flatten it into a rounded patty that's about ¼ inch (6 mm) tall. For best results, construct a mold with a shallow profile. If it's too tall, the clay can rip or stretch too thin.

2. Sprinkle a little talcum powder on the polymer clay patty to prevent the dome form from sticking. Find the center of the patty and press the dome into the center until it touches the table.

3. Cut out the center of the donut shape with the cookie cutter. Carefully press down on the cut edge of the interior circle with your fingertips, forming a knife-edge. You may have to use the cookie cutter once more to regain the circular shape.

4. Use the PVC rolling pin to flatten the outside perimeter of the polymer clay to a knife-edge. Bake the polymer clay on a cookie sheet in the oven, following the manufacturer's instructions for temperature and timing. Use proper ventilation when baking. Let the polymer form cool.

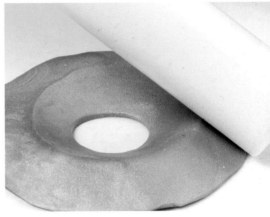

5. Place a sheet of 180-grit emery paper on a flat tabletop. Sand the flat side of the polymer donut until it is completely flush with the tabletop. The inside and the outside edges should be sharp. The interior hole and the outside edge of the circle should be concentric and symmetrical. File as needed, keeping the knife-edges.

6. Prepare a sheet of textured metal clay that's two cards thick and large enough to cover the donut (about 2½ inches [6.4 cm] in diameter). In the exact center of the textured sheet, cut out a circle that's ⅝ inch (1.6 cm) in diameter.

(continued on next page)

7. Drape the textured sheet over the donut mold, lining up the center holes. Gently coax the sheet to conform to the mold. In order to prevent crimping and folding, trim the excess clay to a closer dimension to the mold. The clay edges should touch the table surface and cover the mold. Let the clay dry, and then remove it from the mold.

8. Repeat steps 6 and 7 to make the second side of the bead.

9. When both components are dry, use the 220-grit emery paper to sand both sides of the bead so that they fit flush without significant gaps. Rotate the two sides to find the best fit and make registration marks on both sides at that point.

10. Glue the two sides of the bead together with a generous amount of thick slip, gently pressing them together so the two sides are very close with no gaps. Let the bead dry. Groom the seam by removing excess slip and caulking any gaps. Set aside to dry.

11. Use a carving tool or a craft knife to finish the seam and make a smooth, textural transition between the two sides of the bead. Use a damp paintbrush to remove any tool marks and blend the texture.

12. Place the bead on support material and fire. Finish as desired.

Variations

• Try making different shapes.

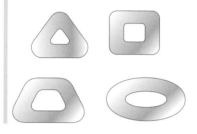

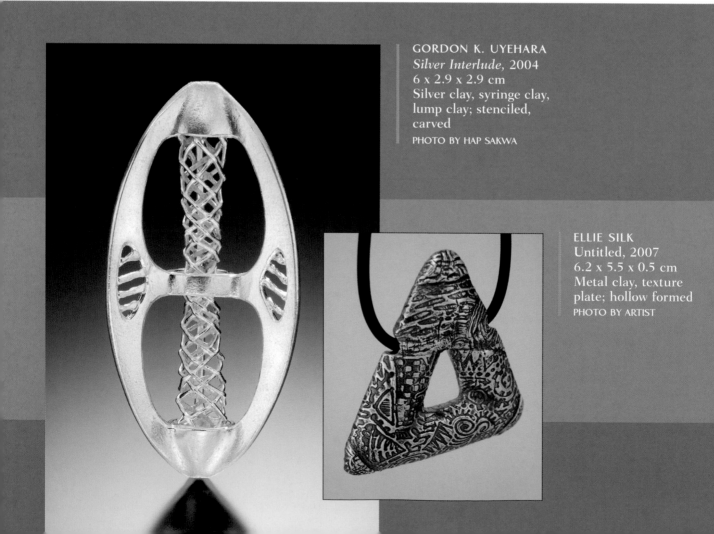

GORDON K. UYEHARA
Silver Interlude, 2004
6 x 2.9 x 2.9 cm
Silver clay, syringe clay, lump clay; stenciled, carved
PHOTO BY HAP SAKWA

ELLIE SILK
Untitled, 2007
6.2 x 5.5 x 0.5 cm
Metal clay, texture plate; hollow formed
PHOTO BY ARTIST

  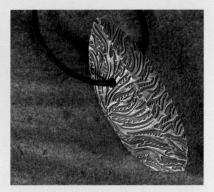

BOX
BEADS

The next four beads are created from dry, flat, textured metal clay sheets. Complex construction with dry metal clay can result in spectacular forms that would be labor-intensive using traditional metalworking methods.

BASIC BOX BEAD

Although the fabrication methods for this bead are basic, the effects created by texture plates can be anything but. If you miter the edges precisely, the textures will blend into one another at the joints for a seamless look. The bead shown is a shallow rectangle, but any variation on a cube is possible because the technique is the same. Making a rough plan of your dimensions will facilitate the process.

MATERIALS

Metal clay
Slip

TOOLS

Basic Tool Kit (page 12)
Texture plates of your choice
Facial or bathroom tissue, one-ply
Emery paper, 220 grit
Half-round needle file, #2 cut
(optional)

STEP BY STEP

1. Decide on the dimensions of your box bead: height, width, and depth. Choose one or more texture plates. Prepare a two-card-thick textured metal clay sheet to make the six sides of the box.

2. Place a piece of one-ply tissue on a flat surface. Peel the textured clay off the plate and place it on the tissue to air-dry. Monitor the drying process from time to time, and gently pat down any warped or buckled spots.

3. Using the depth of your box as a guide, cut four pieces of textured metal clay for the frame: one for the top, one for the bottom, and one for each side. Hold the two longest strips of clay (the sides of the frame) back to back. Use an emery board to file

the narrow ends of the strips to 90° angles. Continue filing until the two pieces match in length. Repeat this process to file the short strips. Don't file the long sides of these strips yet.

4. Working on the nontextured side of the metal clay strips, use an emery board to miter the short sides to a 45° angle, sharp knife-edge. **Important:** If the edge is not taken down to a true, sharp, knife-edge, the seams will not look neat.

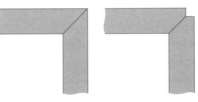

CORRECT   INCORRECT

Take one short strip and one long strip and join them at a 90° angle with slip. Repeat this process to join the two remaining strips. Let both forms dry.

5. Reinforce the inner seam areas of the two L-shaped components with clay, and let them dry. Connect the two components with slip. Caulk and reinforce the remaining seams and allow them to dry. Now the frame for the box bead is complete.

6. Choose one edge of the frame and sweep it back and forth on a sheet of emery paper until it is even and flush with the tabletop. Using the sharp tip of a craft knife or the half-round needle file, miter this edge to a 45° angle, being sure to cut the excess metal clay from the reinforced corners.

(continued on next page)

7. Using a pencil, make a registration mark such as an arrow on one inside edge of the mitered frame. Place the frame mitered-edge side down on the nontextured side of the metal clay sheet. Using a very sharp pencil, trace around the outside of the frame. Before lifting the frame, make a corresponding registration arrow on the metal clay sheet. These registration marks will help you fit the "plates" (the front and back panels of the box bead) to the frame.

8. Using the tip of a craft knife, cut on the pencil mark to create the first "plate." Using your fingers as a gentle vice, hold the plate to the frame. Carefully trim away any excess metal clay with the tip of the craft knife.

9. Use an emery board to file all the nontextured edges of the plate to a 45° knife-edge. Using the registration marks, correctly orient the sides and fit the plate to the frame. If the plate doesn't drop down completely into the frame, see where the metal clay needs further mitering and remove any excess clay.

10. When a good fit is achieved, connect the plate to the frame with a generous amount of thick slip. Let this dry. Reinforce the inner seams with clay, and allow them to dry.

11. Repeat steps 6 through 10 to create the second plate and attach it to the frame. When connecting the second plate, be sure to use a good amount of thick slip because you won't be able to caulk the inner seams.

12. Clean the seams on the box, flicking away oozed slip and caulking any gaps with clay. Let dry. Groom and finish the edges so that the texture from one side of the seam flows into the texture on the other side of the seam. Don't be afraid to add or subtract clay or to create new texture to make this work.

Note: The Basic Box Bead pictured has a fine line of syringe clay piped on top of the seams of the two plates. This option enhances the framelike quality.

13. Smooth all the seam edges with a damp paintbrush. Decide where to place the holes on the bead. Drill the holes and clean any ragged edges around them. Lay the bead flat on a kiln shelf to fire. Finish as desired.

Variation

- Create a different form by letting the plate(s) overhang the frame, like eaves on a roof. For this option, no mitering is required to attach the plate to the frame.

COLLEEN J. STELLA
Cubic Leaf, 2007
1.7 x 1.7 x 1.7 cm
Metal clay, hollow bead, enamel;
constructed, kum boo
PHOTO BY ARTIST

ABOVE

KATHLEEN BOLAN
Squiggle Beads, 2002
1.8 x 1.8 x 1.8 cm
24-karat gold and silver PMC, textured,
appliquéd, patina; hollow core
PHOTO BY TIM THAYER

RIGHT

MARIA MARTINEZ
Imagine, 2007
10.2 x 1.6 x 1.3 cm
Metal clay, sterling silver wire, red coral,
glass beads; hand constructed
PHOTO BY DAVID CASTELLANOS

POLYGON BOX BEAD

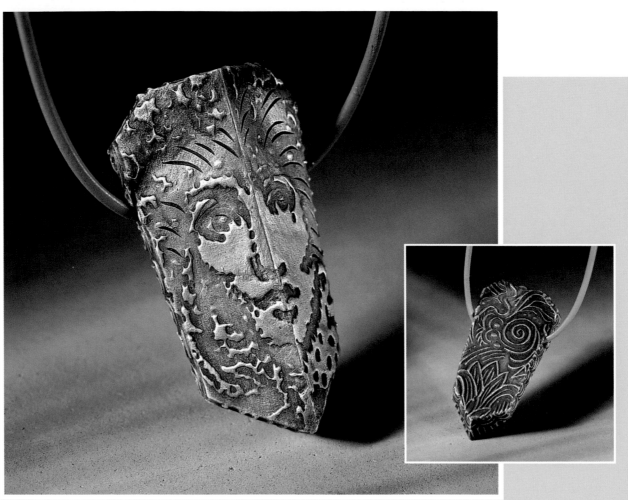

Creating a box bead with more than six planes results in dynamic forms reminiscent of crystals, such as quartz. The most interesting aspect of this bead is the image of the fractured face and the unusual tapering from top to bottom. Its slightly more complex construction process will pose an enjoyable challenge.

MATERIALS

Metal clay
Polymer clay
Slip

TOOLS

Basic Tool Kit (page 12)
3 texture plates of your choice:
  one for the face, two for the
  back and sides of the bead

STEP BY STEP

1. Prepare textured metal clay sheets for the front plate (the face), the frame, and the back plate of the bead. Let the sheets dry completely flat.

2. With the image of the face centered, cut out a rectangular piece of the textured clay for the front plate. Using a ruler, mark a centerline that runs from the top of the plate, through the center of the nose, to the bottom of the plate. Score this line with a craft knife. Cut and separate the two sides of the face.

3. Use an emery board to miter the nontextured edge of the line cut in step 2. Make the mitered knife-edge a 55° angle. This angle is wider than usual so that more of the face will be seen.

4. To set up a drying jig for this unusual angle, press a pat of polymer clay on the tabletop. Hold the two halves of the front plate together at the desired angle. Place one side edge against the polymer clay. Press another piece of polymer to the table, to hold up the two pieces. Remove the metal clay, leaving the polymer in place.

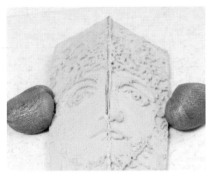

5. Connect the mitered edges of the front plate with slip and place it on the polymer clay jig to dry. Caulk the inner seam of the plate with clay, and allow it to dry. File all seven edges flat with an emery board. Miter all seven nontextured edges. This unfired, angled plate is approximately 1 inch wide (2.5 cm) at the top by 2 inches (5.1 cm) long; it tapers to ⅝ inch (1.5 cm) at the bottom.

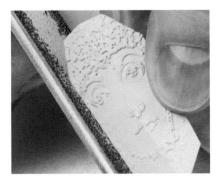

Note: Because this bead tapers from deep at the top to shallow at the bottom, you will begin building the frame at the top and work your way around the box.

6. To create the top section of the frame, cut a strip of dry metal clay sheet that is ⅝ inch (1.6 cm) wide. Make the strip about 2 inches (5.1 cm) long so several frame sections can be cut from it. Use an emery board to file one short edge of the strip at a 90° angle. Lay the metal clay strip on its textured side and place the angled face component on the nontextured side.

7. Use a sharp pencil to trace the angled outline, marked as A, B, C, and D, and remove the angled face component. Draw two lines from the ends of the angle to the edge of the strip, A to D and C to E.

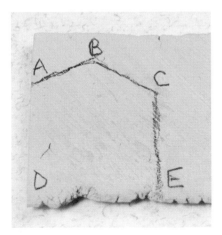

8. Cut out the pentagon shape and miter the untextured side of the four edges: DA, AB, BC, and CE. Fit the angled edges of the side facet to the top angle of the faceplate and tack with slip. Let dry, using another polymer clay jig if necessary. Caulk the inner seam with clay for strength. Let it dry.

9. Proceeding clockwise as you view the top faceplate, make measurements for the next side facet. File the end of the ⅝-inch (1.6 cm) strip to a 90° angle and miter the nontextured edge. Label this edge FG.

10. Place the strip texture-side down and line up edge CE of the previous facet with edge FG. Use a sharp pencil to trace the outline of the top angle, GH.

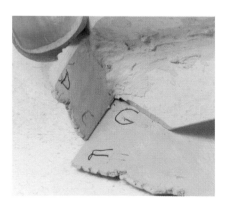

11. Remove the faceplate and draw a line from point H straight to the bottom of the strip, HI. Cut out this shape. Miter edges FG, GH and HI. Hold this piece up to the faceplate next to the first affixed side facet and assess the fit, adjusting if necessary.

12. Once the fit is satisfactory, attach with slip and let the facet dry. Caulk the three inner seams with clay for strength. Continue all the way around the faceplate, fitting, attaching, and caulking each of the five remaining facets.

13. The bottom edge of the facet side plates will be quite irregular. To make it even and flush to the tabletop, sweep it back and forth on the emery sheet. To make it taper from top to bottom, as you are sweeping, press more strongly on the lower part of the faceplate. Take the tip of a craft knife and miter the untextured edges of this seven-sided frame in preparation for setting in the back plate.

14. Lay the back plate textured-side down and set the seven-sided component on top of it. Trace around the shape with a sharp pencil. Cut out the shape and miter the untex-

tured edges. Fit the back plate to the bead and check the fit, cutting away any excess overhang and remitering as needed. When the back plate drops into the bead with a flush fit, secure it with a generous amount of thick slip, and let it dry.

15. Groom all sixteen seams by removing excess slip that has oozed out, and caulk any gaps with clay. Once dry, finish the seams to make the textures flow from one facet to another, and smooth the seams with a damp paintbrush.

16. Determine where the holes should be, and drill accordingly. Groom the holes so no ragged edges remain. Fire flat on a kiln shelf, and finish as desired.

Variation

• Create a three- or four-sided pyramid for the top plate.

• Eliminate the side facets.

• Construct the polygon box bead facet-by-facet to create interesting structures, such as asymmetrical, multisided hollow forms.

CHAIN LINK BEAD

This is a box with two sets of side frames—one on the exterior, and one on the interior. For visual contrast, I add a gold paste product to the inside opening. You can make the link in any shape or size, and even connect two or more if you're feeling especially daring.

MATERIALS

Metal clay
Slip
Gold paste
Liver of sulfur

TOOLS

Basic Tool Kit (page 12)
Texture plate of your choice
Brush for gold paste
Tumbler, shot, and burnishing
    compound

STEP BY STEP

1. Prepare the textured metal clay sheet. For the bead shown, the finished dimensions are 2 x 1⅜ inches (5.1 x 3.5 cm), and it tapers in depth from ³⁄₁₆ inch (5 mm) at the top to ⅜ inch (1 cm) at the bottom. You'll need to make enough flat, dry textured metal clay sheets for the outer frame, the inner frame, and the two plates. Make your sheets larger in dimension than the finished piece so you have enough construction material.

2. Prepare a four-sided, outer frame using the same technique described in the Basic Box Bead project (page 90). File one side of the frame flush with the table. Miter the nontextured edges to 45° angles.

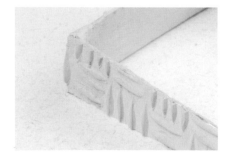

3. With the mitered edges down, place the frame on one of the flat dry sheets designated for the plates. Trace the outline of the frame. Cut out this shape and match it precisely to the frame. Miter the nontextured side of the plate to a 45° angle. Attach the first plate to the frame with thick slip.

4. To build the inner frame, cut out enough dry textured metal clay to provide strips for four sides of the frame. The strips should be the same width as the outer frame. Create the inner frame in the same way you made the outer frame, except miter the corners on the textured side. For the bead shown, the trapezoid has the following dimensions: top, ⅜ inch (1 cm); bottom, ¾ inch (1.9 cm); sides, 1⅛ inches (2.8 cm).

5. When the inner frame is complete, pick one side and file it flush to the tabletop. Miter the nontextured edges to 45° angles. Lay the inner frame inside the outer frame and determine the best placement. In the project bead shown, the top of the little trapezoid is ⅜ inch (1 cm) from the top of the outer bead edge.

6. Use a sharp pencil to trace inside the outline of the trapezoid. Use the tip of a craft knife and cut away the excess metal clay to open up a trapezoid-shaped hole in the plate. Miter the nontextured edges of the hole to 45° angles. Fit the inner frame to this hole. Once the fit is precise, attach with slip. Set aside to dry.

7. Caulk clay into the nontextured side of both the inner and outer frames. Let dry. To taper the bead from top to bottom, sweep the open edges of the bead back and forth on the emery sheet, bearing down more heavily on the top edge. If you don't want to taper your bead, file it with even pressure. Check to see whether the edges fit flush to the tabletop, and make sure there are no gaps.

8. Miter the nontextured sides of the inner and the outer frames by carefully carving with a craft knife. Prepare a large sheet of textured metal clay and set aside to dry. Lay the entire bead (inner and outer frames connected to the first plate) edge-side down on the nontextured side of the large, dry sheet. Trace around the outside of the outer frame and the inside hole of the inner frame with a sharp pencil. Cut out this shape and miter the nontextured edges.

9. Check the fit of the second plate to the mitered edges and adjust as needed. Attach the mitered edges together with slip, and set aside to dry. Clean and groom all seams.

10. Use the inner frame as the "hole" for the bead, or drill a hole, if desired. Fire the bead flat on a kiln shelf.

11. Follow the manufacturer's directions for adding the gold paste to the inner frame of the bead. To achieve the gunmetal look of the bead shown, tumble it to a mirror finish and then dip it in hot liver of sulfur. (Don't remove any of the patina chemicals.)

Variation

- Both the outer and the inner frames can vary in shape.
- With different frames you can make hollow interlinked forms.

1. Make the first hollow box and fire it.
2. Completely construct and finish the second box.
3. Use a jewelers' saw to cut the hollow link apart.
4. Link it to the previously fired box, and then reconstruct the seam to disguise where it was sawn apart.
5. Fire the second link.
6. Continue this process to make as many links as desired.

TOP
BARBARA BECKER SIMON
Big Links, 2006
50 cm long
Fine silver, stainless steel, sterling silver; interconnected hollow links
PHOTO BY LARRY SANDERS

BOTTOM
BARBARA BECKER SIMON
Picture Frame Box Ring, 2006
3.5 x 3 x 3.5 cm
Fine silver, cubic zirconia, fine gold; kum boo, stone setting
PHOTO BY LARRY SANDERS

LEMON WEDGE BEAD

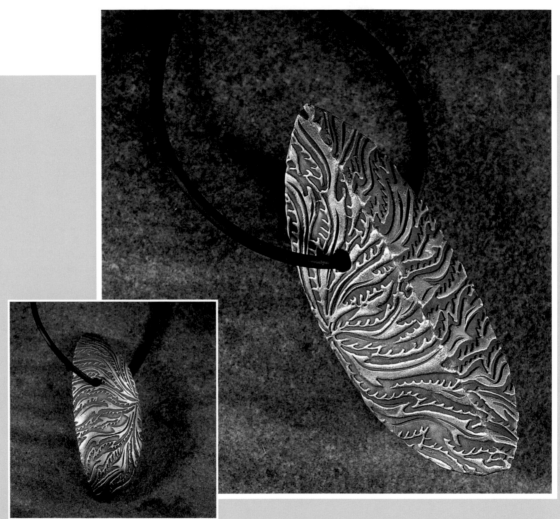

This slice of a bead combines curved and flat dry metal clay textured with botanically inspired designs. I molded it over a plastic jellybean box. You can find a similar box by searching online, or by looking in the plastic egg container section when retail stores have their Easter displays up.

MATERIALS

Metal clay
Slip

TOOLS

Basic Tool Kit (page 12)
Texture plate of your choice
Plastic jellybean mold form or
  similar mold shape made from
  polymer clay
Emery paper, 220 grit

STEP BY STEP

1. Create a sheet of textured metal clay two cards thick that measures 2 x ¾ inches (5.1 x 1.9 cm). Lightly oil the mold, and choose a texture plate. A radial design texture plate looks particularly nice on the curved portion of this bead.

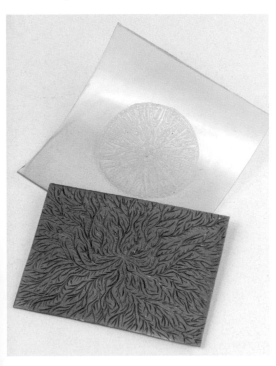

2. Drape the metal clay on the form, coaxing the wet sheet to the contours of the plastic. To facilitate the draping, cut off any excess clay, and dry the clay on the form. Cut or file the shape on one side only. Miter the filed nontextured edge.

3. Lay the mitered edge on the nontextured side of one of the flat dry textured metal clay sheets. With a sharp pencil, trace outside the curved edge on the flat sheet. Cut on the pencil line, continuing the curve. There will be excess metal clay, which will be eliminated later on.

4. Miter the nontextured, curved edge of the flat sheet and fit it to the molded, curved component, filing and remitering until the two fit together with a knife-edge.

5. Glue the two pieces together with slip, and allow it to dry. Caulk the inner seam with clay for strength. Once dry, eliminate any excess

material by drawing a line on the flat sheet between the points of the curved component. Score with a knife and break the excess off.

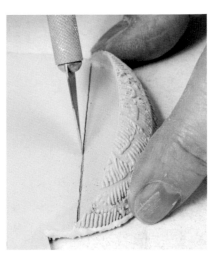

6. Trim the other side of the curved component to determine the size of the bead. To remove a small amount of clay, use an emery board; to remove a large amount, score and break the clay.

7. Place the bead edge-side down on a sheet of 220-grit emery paper and file the edges so they are flush with the table. Miter these nontextured edges to a knife-edge.

8. Place the second flat, dry, textured metal clay sheet texture-side down. Lay the bead mitered-edge down on the flat sheet and trace around the form with a sharp pencil.

9. Cut out this shape and miter and file the edges until you can fit the third side of the bead into the form so that it drops in and forms knife-edges. Secure the third side with generous amounts of thick slip.

(continued on next page)

10. Once dry, groom and clean the seam, caulking any gaps with clay. By adding or subtracting clay, make the textured surfaces flow on each side of the seam. Finish the seams with a damp paintbrush. Drill the holes for the bead and clean any ragged edges. Fire the bead supported with vermiculite or a fiber blanket. Finish as desired.

Variation

- Cut the bead apart to make more than one bead, and cap the open ends with a flat metal clay sheet.

- Instead of filing the last edges flat and flush to the tabletop, use an emery board to curve the profile. Cap this curve with a sheet of wet textured metal clay. This bead will have two curved sides.

- Truncate the ends of the bead by cutting off the tips and capping it with a flat metal clay sheet.

LEFT
BARBARA BECKER SIMON
Red Rocks, 2005
Largest, 5 x 3 x 1.5 cm
Fine silver, stainless steel, granite, basalt, sterling silver; hollow box beads
PHOTO BY LARRY SANDERS

BELOW
ANGELA B. CRISPIN
Now Paint the Town Red,
Urban-Ethnic™ Series, 2007
7.5 x 2.5 x 1 cm
Metal clay, faux bone; box construction, hand carved, oxidized, hand sawed, drilled, carved, sanded, heat formed
PHOTO BY ARTIST

DRAPED
BEADS

This type of bead involves hanging wet clay over an armature and letting it dry. This dry-draped form dictates the shape of the rest of the bead. The additional sides of the bead may be connected in dry or wet form.

103

TABLE EDGE BEAD

At first glance, you might not recognize the source of this bead's interesting shape: it comes from draping wet textured clay over the edge of a table. Use your imagination to rig up all sorts of "landscapes" over which to drape clay, using common objects taped or otherwise adhered to a work surface.

MATERIALS

Metal clay
Cubic zirconia gemstones (optional)
Slip
Gold for kum boo or gold paste
    (optional)
Liver of sulfur

TOOLS

Basic Tool Kit (page 12)
Bamboo skewer, chopstick, drink
    stirrer, or similar rod
Texture plate of your choice
Glass jar or tumbler
Brush for gold (optional)

STEP BY STEP

1. Tape the skewer to the table about ⅛ inch (3 mm) parallel from the edge.

2. For the first draped side, make a two-card-thick textured sheet of metal clay that measures 2 x 1¾ inches (5.1 x 4.4 cm). Drape this sheet over the skewer and the table edge.

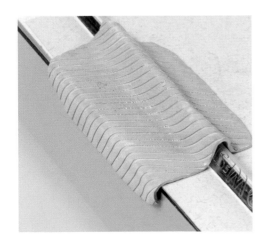

3. Gently press the wet clay into the depression between the skewer and the table edge, to create a concave fold. While the wet clay is draped, press in the cubic zirconia gemstones so that the tables of the stones are below the surface of the metal clay. Let dry.

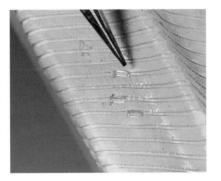

4. Prepare another texture sheet two cards thick that measures 3 x 1 inches (7.6 x 2.5 cm). Drape this sheet lengthwise on a lightly oiled jar or tumbler to create a gentle curve. Let it dry.

5. To create the top piece of the bead, roll out a texture sheet to four cards thick and cut out a 1-inch (2.5 cm) square. Allow this to dry.

6. File the edges of the draped piece to achieve the final shape, and miter the two long edges. Take the dried metal clay sheet off the jar and place it on its textured side. Place the draped piece on top of the nontextured side of the jar piece, toward one end, so that the excess can be used for the bottom of the bead.

7. With a sharp pencil, trace the outline of the draped piece on the nontextured side of the jar piece. Using a craft knife, cut out the curved back piece. Miter the two long sides of the jar piece so that they fit flush to the two long mitered sides of the draped piece.

8. Glue the two sides together using a generous amount of thick slip. Let this dry. Caulk the inner seams with clay for reinforcement. Once dry, use the remaining curved piece as a guide to file the corresponding curve on the bottom of the bead.

(continued on next page)

9. Miter the inside edge of the bottom of the bead. Lay the curved piece on the bottom of the bead and trace the outline with a sharp pencil. Cut out the shape and miter the edges. When they fit, glue the pieces together with thick slip.

10. Once it is dry, file the left-hand seam of the bead flat. Pierce to create the area for the gold. It may take some filing or another flat plate to achieve the small, flat edge.

11. File the top piece with an emery board so that the top edge is a 90° angle. Because this piece is sitting on top with an overhang, there is no need to miter. Glue the pieces together with thick slip and let this dry.

12. Clean up all seam areas by removing oozed slip and caulking any gaps with clay. Once dry, groom the seams to make the textures flow back and forth from one plane to the next. Finish the seams with a damp paintbrush.

13. Drill and clean up the holes. Fire the bead supported with vermiculite or a fiber blanket. If using gold paste or kum boo, make sure you don't touch that area with your fingers when handling the bead. When using patina, use liver of sulfur to avoid coloring the gold.

WIRE ARMATURE BEAD

Almost any but the thinnest gauge of wire can be used to create the armature over which to drape the clay for this bead. My version has a visually interesting impressed texture accented with kum boo, but it would also look great using texture plates, and you can opt out of adding the gold foil.

MATERIALS

12 inches (30.5 cm) of 16-, 14-, 12-, 10-, or 8-gauge copper wire or similar (do not use aluminum wire)
Metal clay
Slip
Gold for kum boo (optional)
Liver of sulfur

TOOLS

Basic Tool Kit (page 12)
Wire nippers
Emery paper, 220 grit
Brush for gold
Pliers (optional)

STEP BY STEP

1. Using wire nippers, bend the wire into a simple form that will rest easily on the tabletop. Lightly oil the wire.

2. Roll out a piece of metal clay sheet two cards thick that measures 2¼ x 2 inches (5.7 x 5.1 cm). Impress the wet clay with a needle tool, a stiff toothbrush, or another tool of your choice to create the tiny dot pattern.

3. Drape the metal clay over the wire armature, gently pressing it with your fingertips to conform to the contours of the wire. Cut off any excess clay at this time.

4. Roll out another piece of metal clay two cards thick and texture it in the same way. Let this dry flat.

5. Sweep the edges of the dry-draped piece on a sheet of 220-grit emery paper so that the edges are flush to the table. Miter the edges.

Note: Depending on the manner in which the clay was draped over the wire, all edges may not end up being flush. So once the back plate is attached, any open areas can be capped to make an interesting form. The bead in this project has two areas where the flat sheet and the curvature of the draped piece did not meet.

6. Lay the draped piece on top of the nontextured side of the flat piece and trace the outline with a sharp pencil. Cut out this shape, fit it to the draped piece, and miter the edges. Glue with a generous amount of thick slip and let it dry.

7. Using pieces of dry flat sheet or draping with wet sheet, cap off any openings that the back did not cover. Clean the seams and caulk any gaps with clay. Let this dry. Groom the seams to a neat edge, finishing with a damp paintbrush.

8. Drill and clean the holes, and fire it flat on a kiln shelf.

9. If you wish to kum boo the piece after firing, be careful not to touch the areas to be covered with gold paste or gold. To patina, use liver of sulfur so as to not color the gold.

Variation

- File the outer edge of the dry draped component so that it's not flat. This means you'll have to fit the back of the bead by draping, and then glue a wet sheet of metal clay to the dry side with slip.

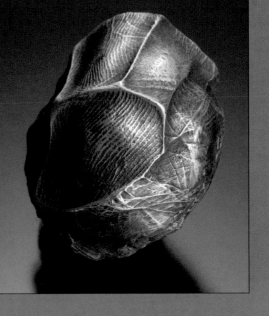

TOP
ANNE LINGENER-REECE
Long Leaf Necklace, Falling Leaf Series, 2007
28 x 14 x 1.5 cm
Fine silver mesh, metal clay, aquamarine
rundell beads, cultured pearl, antique black
background, pear blue/green tourmaline;
hand formed, embellished
PHOTO BY ARTIST

RIGHT
TIM MCCREIGHT
Untitled, 2006
2.8 x 1.3 cm
Fine silver; pressed
PHOTO BY ROBERT DIAMANTE

LEFT
CINDY PANKOPF
Crownshaft, 2007
3.5 x 3 x 3 cm
Art clay silver, metal clay
veneer, cork clay, overlay paste
PHOTO BY ARTIST

SHEET METAL
ARMATURE BEAD

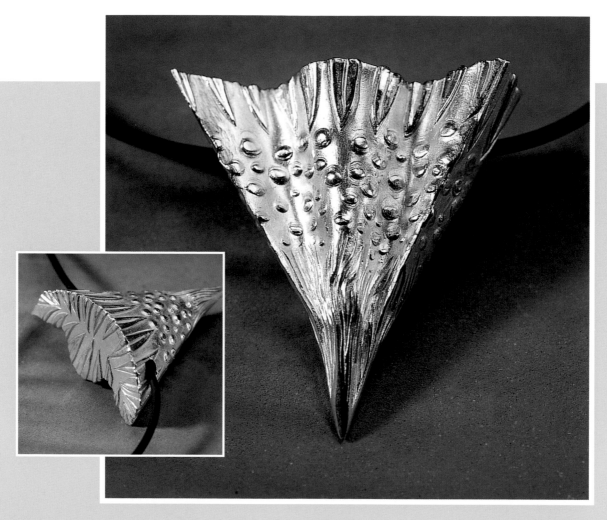

In this project, you'll bend a thin sheet of copper into a support for the drying clay. This single armature is very versatile, because you can drape clay over it in a variety of ways.

MATERIALS

Copper sheet, 28 gauge
Metal clay
Slip
Polymer clay

TOOLS

Basic Tool Kit (page 12)
Tin snips or shears
Texture plate(s) of your choice
Emery paper, 220 grit
Pliers (optional)

STEP BY STEP

Note: This project uses two sheet metal forms, one for the wavy front and another for the curved back.

1. Using tin snips, create the armatures for the front and the back of the bead, using a 4 x 2-inch (10.2 x 5.1 cm) flat sheet of thin copper for each. Bend them in such a way that they sit securely on the table. Lightly oil the surface of each armature.

2. Roll out a textured sheet of metal clay to the thickness of two cards. Drape it over the armature, starting in the middle of the wet sheet and working through to the ends. This will be the front of the bead.

Note: This technique makes it easier to fit the wet sheet into the contours of the armature without stretching the clay.

3. Trim the excess clay from this piece to form the outline of the bead.

4. Roll out another textured sheet of metal clay and drape it over the armature. This will be the back of the bead.

5. Refine the triangular shape of the front wavy component using an emery board.

6. Prepare two flat plates of metal clay that are roughly rectangular for the sides of the bead and dry flat.

7. On one of the long sides of these flat plates, create a straight edge by scoring and breaking.

8. Line up one straight side of the front piece along the straight edge of the side piece. Mark with a pencil where the flat piece extends beyond the back piece to find the length of the side piece. Cut off the excess.

9. Determine the width of the side piece. This piece should look like an elongated trapezoid. Measure and cut away the excess.

10. Miter the straight edges of both the side and the front pieces.

11. Use thick slip to attach the flat side panels to the curved piece. If needed, use polymer clay to help set it up to dry. Caulk the inner seam with clay and repeat the process for the other side panel.

12. When both side panels are secure, sweep the form on a sheet of 220-grit emery paper to refine the edges. Miter the two side panel edges.

13. Fit the front piece to the back piece by tracing the outline of the front shape on the nontextured side of the back piece. Cut out this shape.

(continued on next page)

14. Fit the side panels to the back piece by mitering and filing until the back curved piece drops into the front piece with a knife-edge. Glue the panels together with thick slip. Caulk the seams and let them dry.

15. File the top edge until it is even, and then miter it. Trace the top to the nontextured side of the flat dry metal clay piece. Cut out this shape. Miter and file it until it fits the top piece. Attach it with thick slip.

16. Roll some metal clay into a rough cone shape and attach it to the bottom of the taper with thick slip. Don't worry if the cone is too big—you can file and groom it when it is dry.

17. To blend the cone shape to the body of the bead, file, carve, and caulk as needed. Clean and groom all seams so that the textures flow from one plane to the next. Use a carving tool to blend the texture into the cone-shaped cap.

18. Drill and clean the holes. Fire supported with vermiculite or a fiber blanket. Finish as desired.

Variation

- Use heavy Manila paper instead of metal to create a form.

- Use both sides of the armature to create a form.

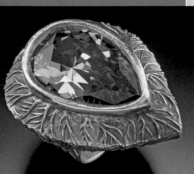

BEADS WITH
SOMETHING EXTRA

These next seven projects have a little added attraction, such as enameling, using resin, implanting wire, and combining metal clay with lampworked glass. Most are constructed with techniques that have been covered in previous projects, but I've included new materials and more complex constructions to challenge your skills.

ENAMELED BEAD

Enameling can be taken to complex places, but for this project you'll learn a very simple, basic champlevé technique that nonetheless yields exquisite results. The enamels are positioned in the depression by wet packing, laid from dark to light to create an *ombré* effect. Although my bead features enameling on both faces, you can simplify the project by embellishing only one side.

MATERIALS

Metal clay
Slip
Ammonia
Transparent turquoise enamel in
  light, medium, and dark
Transparent purple enamel in light,
  medium, and dark
Distilled water

TOOLS

Basic Tool Kit (page 12)
Small rubber stamp
Texturing tools
Slightly domed mold
Emery paper, 220 grit
Texture plate of your choice
  (optional)
Copper wire, 8 gauge
Tumbler, stainless steel mixed shot,
  and burnishing compound
Dust mask
Small plastic drinking cups
Marker
Small spatula for packing enamels
Enameling trivet or grid
Enameling fork
Mold for forming the sides

Note: If you've never enameled
before, practice on little test tiles of
fine sheet silver before beginning the
project.

STEP BY STEP

1. Choose a simple rubber stamp
that is less than 1 inch (2.5 cm)
long, with plenty of open space to
pack with enamels. Steer away from
stamps with a lot of lines or texture.

2. Imprint the stamp on a piece
of paper and draw a template for
the faceplates of your bead. Leave a
¼-inch (6 mm) border between the
edge of the stamp and the faceplate.
Placing enamels too close to the edge
of a shape may result in cracking.

3. Roll out a sheet of metal clay six
cards thick. Press your stamp into
the clay to create an even, shallow
imprint for each of your faceplates.
You don't want to create too deep
a depression, or the enamel might
crack. Cut out the faceplates and
decorate them with texturing tools.

4. Select or create a mold that's
slightly domed, and lightly oil it.
Place the faceplates on the mold
and allow them to dry. **Note:** Doming
the faceplate will counteract the
tension of the fired enamels so you
won't have to employ a counter-
enameling step.

5. Referring to your template, sweep
the edges of the domed faceplates on
a sheet of 220-grit emery paper, being
careful to maintain a ¼-inch (6 mm)
border around your stamped design.
Match the two domes together so
they're the same size and shape. With
your pencil, make a registration mark
on the perimeter of the domes. Mark
one as dome A and one as dome B, to
avoid confusion later.

6. Place dome A on a piece of paper
and trace its outline using a sharp
pencil. Make a registration mark
somewhere on the edge of the tracing
that matches the mark on the dome.

7. Place a piece of acetate paper
over the tracing. On a piece of paper,
cut a strip that's ⅜ inch (1 cm) wide
and 6 inches (15.2 cm) long. Wrap
this strip around the tracing and
mark where the ends meet with a
pencil. Add ½ inch (1.3 cm) to the
length of the paper to provide enough
overlap to make the seam. This paper
template strip will be used to make
the side of the bead.

(continued on next page)

8. Using the template strip as a guide, roll out a long sheet of metal clay three cards thick. Cut out the side strip and texture it, if desired. Wrap the long edge of the side strip on top of the acetate using the pencil outline as a guide. **Note:** Be sure to place the outside edge of the clay strip *inside* the pencil mark, otherwise the band may be too big. With a sharp craft knife, slice through the overlapped ends to discard the excess clay and create the butt seam.

9. Double-check that the clay strip mimics the pencil outline, and then glue the ends together with slip. The clay will be a little floppy, but if you continue to work with it, you can get it to stay upright to form a band. Let it dry on the acetate. (Drying it directly on the paper will cause the clay to buckle.) Before removing the band from the acetate, make a registration mark on the band that corresponds to the line made in step 5 on dome A, and to the registration mark on the tracing made in step 6.

10. Clean any oozed slip from the inside of the seam, and caulk with clay. Leave the outer seam for later.

11. Once dry, make note of the edge of the band with the registration mark and even it out by sweeping that edge across a sheet of emery paper or an emery board. Fit the registration mark on the band together with the mark on dome A to help you judge the fit between the two pieces. Depending on the type of texture used, you can choose whether or not to miter. Secure the two pieces together with thick slip.

12. Once dry, caulk the inner seam with clay. Repeat the process for attaching dome B, making and matching a new corresponding registration mark on the open edge of the band to fit the last side of the bead. Groom the seams by cleaning oozed slip and caulking any gaps with clay. Add and subtract clay as needed to make the seams invisible.

13. Finish grooming with a damp paintbrush applied to the seam areas. Drill and clean the holes. Fire the bead with vermiculite or a fiber blanket for support.

14. Thread a piece of 8-gauge copper wire through the bead holes and bend the ends so the bead will not slip off. This will prevent any stainless steel shot from getting trapped inside the bead. Place the bead in the tumbler for 2 to 3 hours, and check until a mirror finish is achieved. **Note:** A very high polish and a burnishing of the stamped area are necessary to make the metal sparkle through the layer of transparent enamel.

15. Rinse your bead with soap and water. It is important not to have any soap or grease residue on any area of the bead. A final rinse with a solution of 80% ammonia and 20% water is optimum. Allow the bead to dry, and don't touch the area where the enamels will be placed.

Champlevé Enameling

Champlevé is French for "raised plain" or "field." Traditionally, the metal is etched, but for this project the depression is stamped in the metal clay, and then filled with transparent enamels.

Preparing the Enamel

1. Select the color you'd like to use. Using a dust mask, place ⅛ teaspoon of the darkest enamel in a plastic drinking cup. Use a marker to label the cup with the type of enamel.

2. Fill the cup halfway with tap water and swirl the water around for about 5 seconds. The finer, powdery particles of the enamel will float to the top. Carefully pour this water out. The enamel, being heavier, will stay on the bottom. Repeat this step.

3. Repeat the rinsing a third time using distilled water. When pouring out the distilled water, leave a little water in the cup. Set this cup aside and repeat the process with the other two shades of enamel.

Packing the Enamel

1. Lay out a clean sheet of paper on your work surface. With a clean spatula, scoop up a bit of the darkest color. If it is hard to scoop, there is too much water in the cup and you'll need to pour some out.

2. Carefully pack a bit of enamel inside one edge of your stamped area. Clean off the spatula and pack

the medium color next to the dark enamel, taking up about one-third of the space.

3. Clean the spatula and pack the lightest shade in the last third of the space. If you like, you can add more enamel to mound up higher than the surrounding metal.

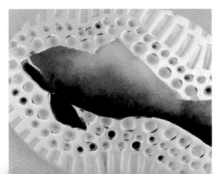

4. Clean off any tiny bits of enamel that have strayed beyond the depression, and allow the water to completely evaporate. Set your digital controller or your manual control on the kiln to 1520°F (827°C).

5. Carefully set the bead on a trivet and place it in the kiln with an enameling fork. If you have a digital control, let the kiln climb back to 1500°F (816°C) and wait 45 seconds.

(continued on next page)

6. Open the door and peek at the piece. The enamel should have a smooth, glossy surface. Using the fork, remove the trivet with the bead and place it on a heat-proof surface. If the enamel surface is bumpy, put it back in the kiln and let the temperature climb back to 1500°F (816°C). Wait 25 seconds.

Note: It is extremely important to be at the kiln at all times during the enameling process. The glass will change quickly and you must remove it as soon as the enamel has flowed.

7. After the enamel has cooled, check the level of the enamel; it should be even with the surrounding metal. If not, pack a bit more enamel into the cavity following the same color sequence. Let this dry and refire.

8. To enamel the other side of the bead, repolish the stamped area by putting it into the tumbler again. Repeat the enameling process using the second color, but suspend the bead in a trivet to avoid damaging the already enameled side. If the enamel touches any surface, it will fuse to that surface.

9. Finish your piece as desired. Feel free to use the tumbler, a brass brush, or patina chemicals. None of these will harm the glass.

TOP
LINDA KAYE-MOSES
River Summer, 2007
69 cm long
Fine silver, sterling silver, vitreous enamel, lapis lazuli, Tibetan turquoise, silk; carved, enameled, patinated
PHOTO BY EVAN J. SOLDINGER

TOP RIGHT
CATHERINE DAVIES PAETZ
Untitled, 2007
1 x 2 x 1 cm
Metal clay, enamel, sterling silver; tube constructed, water etched, enameled, Viking knitted
PHOTO BY ARTIST

BOTTOM
MAGGIE BERGMAN
Untitled, 2007
6 x 1.2 cm
Vitreous enamel, metal clay, photopolymer plate
PHOTO BY J. KUIJSTERS

ALL STONE BEAD

Taking full advantage of peridot's natural ability to withstand the firing schedule, this bead is completely composed of stones, but you could use fewer gems and substitute metal clay elements for a different effect. Use any fire-friendly gemstones or, if you prefer, small pieces of glass.

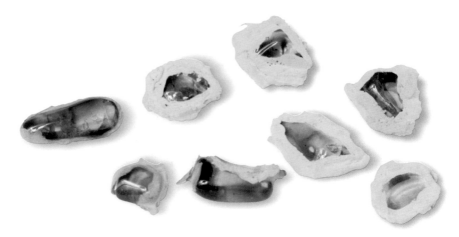

MATERIALS

Tumbled peridot pieces* or small
    bits of glass tumbled or in
    cabochon form
Metal clay slip

TOOLS

Basic Tool Kit (page 12)
Polymer clay
Toothpicks
2 Styrofoam balls, ¾ inch (1.9 cm)
    in diameter
Straight pins

*This bead has 30 to 40 small stones.

STEP BY STEP

1. Put two gumball-size pats of
polymer clay on the table. Stick a
toothpick in each Styrofoam ball and
insert it into the polymer clay.

2. Choose a tumbled stone and
apply metal clay slip around the
widest circumference of the stone.
For the smallest stones, paint as
much of the circumference as
possible, taking breaks to allow it to
dry until you can handle it again and
finish painting all the way around.
Coat each stone with three coats of
slip. Don't worry about covering too
much of the stone—the excess will
be scraped off after several pieces are
"linked" together.

3. Select two stones to begin the
construction process, and place a dab
of slip between the stones to connect
them. Secure these in position with
straight pins on a Styrofoam ball. This
will create the curvature needed to
make the spherical form. Let this dry.

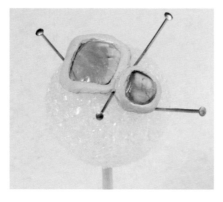

4. Choose two more stones, paste
them together, and position them on
the other Styrofoam ball. When the
first set is dry, caulk the inside seam
with clay. Repeat this process for the
second set of stones.

5. Reposition the first set of stones
on the ball with pins. Select another
stone and secure it with slip to
one or two of the stones. Use pins
to keep it in place. Add two more
stones to the first set in the same
way. Repeat this process for the
second set of stones. When dry,
caulk the insides of all the seams.

6. Continue building each set of
stones and scrape off any excess clay
on the inner surfaces of the form as
you construct the bead. Don't worry
about the excess clay on the outside
of the stones—this will be scraped
and groomed when the bead is
completely formed.

7. As you add stones to each
set, hold the two sides together to
determine the final shape, adding
more stones until you form a sphere.
Don't build the components beyond
the Styrofoam ball's "equator" or you
won't be able to lift them off the
ball. When the two hemispheres are
complete, connect them with heavy
slip and leave them to dry.

8. Clean and groom the outside of the bead, caulking the seams as needed for strength or aesthetic appeal. Scrape away any excess clay so that each stone is displayed but secure in its paste bezel. Fire the bead supported with vermiculite or a fiber blanket. You can use any of the naturally occurring gaps between the stones as holes for your hanging device.

Variation

- Instead of tumbled stones, use cabochons or faceted cuts, or even glass forms, such as marbles or cubes.

- Use mosaic tile or any small pieces of ceramic or glass.
- Use a smaller ratio of implants to metal clay components.

TOP

WENDY WALLIN MALINOW
Hugs and Kisses, 2007
100 cm long
Metal clay, polymer clay, linen; hollow formed, textured, patinated, infilled
PHOTO BY COURTNEY FRISSE

LEFT

ANN DAVIS
Cnidarian (Coval), 2007
6.5 x 2 cm
Lampworked glass and frits, PMC3; slip painted, extruded, incised
PHOTO BY JERRY ANTHONY

BOX IN A BOX BEAD

The fairly complex construction of this bead pays off in the visual punch of the finished object. Inset boxes in each faceplate display an old photograph held simply in place by epoxy resin. (Here, you see a Victorian lady; her beau appears on the other side of the bead.) Epoxies can mimic the more difficult technique of enameling. They can be embedded with small items such as seeds or tiny glass beads to create yet more texture, and can even be tinted.

MATERIALS

Metal clay
Slip

TOOLS

Basic Tool Kit (page 12)
Texture plate of your choice
Emery paper, 220 grit

STEP BY STEP

1. Roll out enough metal clay to make a six-sided basic box bead that's two cards thick. Texture the metal clay as desired and let it dry flat. The faceplates of the bead shown are 7/8 x 1 inch (2.2 x 2.5 cm) long and 5/16 inch (8 mm) wide. Some dry, flat metal clay will be needed for the inner boxes—this can be scrap of any kind because it won't be seen.

Note: For this bead, I used a plastic model of a Victorian building that I bought in the model train section of a hobby store. I used a two-part silicone mold material to make molds of certain sections.

2. Determine the outer dimensions for the faceplates of your bead, accounting for the size and placement of the image you will use. Cut the pieces 1/16 to 1/8 inch (2 to 3 mm) larger to allow for the loss of material due to fitting.

3. Using dry, flat metal clay scrap, cut strips about 1/8 inch (3 mm) wide to create the sides (frames) of the two inner boxes. Refer to the Basic Box Bead or the Chain Link Bead on pages 90 or 97 to create the inner frame construction. Use the dimensions and the shape of your photo to determine the size of the frames.

4. To attach the first inner frame, choose one edge to emery flush, and sweep it on a sheet of 220-grit emery paper. Lay that edge on the nontextured side of one of the faceplates and check for correct placement. Trace inside the frame with a sharp pencil. Apply slip to the faceplate and affix the frame to the faceplate with the filed edge down, using the pencil tracing as a guide for placement.

5. Reinforce the outer seam on the frame with clay. Cut out the metal clay that forms the framed opening on the faceplate. Trim the excess clay so that the seam is neat and tidy, and caulk any gaps. Use an emery board to file the exposed edge of the inner frame flat.

6. To back the little frame, use any piece of dry, flat metal clay scrap that can fit on top of the frame, and attach it to the edge of the frame with slip. Trim any excess clay and clean any oozed slip from the inside of the inset box. Any bumps of excess clay will not allow the photo to sit straight. Repeat this process for the frame on the second faceplate.

7. To make the outer frame that creates the sides of the box, use the technique described in the Basic Box Bead on page 90. The sides of the bead shown are 7/16 inch (1.1 cm) wide. Your strip might need to be wider or narrower based on how much depth the inset boxes occupy. Be sure to leave extra material in the width of this strip so that when the second side of the frame is emeried flat, the second faceplate can drop in. Also, when you plan for the depth of the outside frame, make sure that there is enough room between the two inner boxes for the stringing material to pass through. Cut enough strips for the four sides.

(continued on next page)

8. Make a frame that will fit inside the perimeter of the faceplate. Make sure that it fits the same way on both faceplates. Use an emery on one side of the frame so that it fits flush with the tabletop.

When the frame is fully constructed, position it on the nontextured side of one of the faceplates. With a sharp pencil, trace the outline of the frame on the faceplate. Then, cut away the excess clay.

9. Miter the filed edge of the frame and the corresponding faceplate. Fit the two together, subtracting metal clay so that the faceplate drops into the frame with a knife-edge. Glue the frame and faceplate together with thick slip.

10. Once the slip has dried, caulk the inner seam with clay. Emery the edge of the frame, taking care not to emery the inset box. Lay the edge of the bead frame on the nontextured side of the second faceplate. Trace the outline of the frame onto the clay with a sharp pencil.

11. Remove the excess clay from the second faceplate and miter the edges of the faceplate and the frame. Fit the two together, subtracting metal clay so that the faceplate drops into the frame with a knife-edge. Secure the two components with thick slip.

12. Once the bead is dry, clean and groom the joints for a seamless look. Drill and clean the holes, and fire flat on a kiln shelf. Finish as desired.

ALICE ALPER-REIN
Spinning Beads Kaleidoscope, 2007
Beads, 0.8 x 2.5 x 3.5 cm
Metal clay, 24-karat gold, sterling silver, lab grown sapphire, lab grown ruby; dry constructed, sculpted, textured, kum boo, patinated
PHOTO BY ARTIST

Using UV Curing Epoxy Resin

MATERIALS

- Dental floss
- Photos
- Alcohol
- Cotton swabs
- UV epoxy resin*
- Cup warmer or heating pad
- Butane barbecue lighter
- Toothpicks or small spatula
- UV lamp from a home improvement store or beauty supply store
- UV epoxy resin cleaner (optional)

*You may use two-part epoxy resin (which cures with time) instead of UV epoxy. Familiarize yourself with the manufacturer's instructions, and always test the epoxy resin first. If you make a mistake, there are products that dissolve epoxy so you can try again.

1. Choose one side of the bead to begin working on, and layer 6 inches (15.2 cm) of dental floss across the inset opening to lift the photo in case it gets stuck. Cut the photos to fit inside the boxes. Once the fit is good, remove the floss and clean the opening with alcohol on a cotton swab to remove dirt and oil. Insert the photo in the opening.

2. Place the container of epoxy resin on the cup warmer to raise its temperature. This will allow the epoxy resin to flow better into the opening and help prevent trapped air bubbles. If you find an air bubble, hold the flame of the butane lighter just above the surface of the epoxy; it will draw the bubble to the surface so it can pop.

3. With the bead placed perfectly flat, use a toothpick or small spatula to drop a small amount of epoxy resin on top of the photo, letting the liquid flow over the image. By adding small amounts, you lessen the chance of trapping air bubbles.

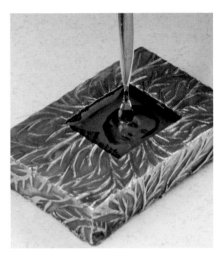

4. Place the bead about 3 inches (7.6 cm) under a UV lightbulb for 1 to 2 minutes.

Remove it from under the lamp and keep adding small amounts of epoxy resin, then curing it under the UV lamp, until the desired depth is reached. Be careful that nothing touches the surface of the resin—no dirt, dust, or fingerprints.

5. Depending on the type of UV resin you use, when the last layer of resin has cured, it will be sticky. Use a cotton swab dipped in the UV resin cleaner to wipe the surface clean of any tackiness. Repeat the process for the other side of the bead.

GLASS SHEET BEAD

Using a variation of the copper foil technique for stained glass, you can easily form the sides of a bead with glass sheet secured between metal clay paper. I embellished the metal clay paper by giving it a pinked edge, but all kinds of scissors that make other decorative cuts are available in craft stores. Any kind of sheet glass will work: window glass, stained glass, fusing glass, or even—as in the case of this bead—microscope slides.

MATERIALS

Glass sheet*
Metal clay
Metal clay paper
Slip
Syringe metal clay

TOOLS

Basic Tool Kit (page 12)
Glass cutter
Texture plate or some strips of
   flat, dry, textured metal clay
Decorative scissors (optional)

*Regular window (float) glass can be used, but it will turn yellowish after firing due to the contact with silver. Certain types of colorless clear fusing glass and microscope slide glass are unaffected by contact with silver.

Note: The finished dimensions of the bead are 1⅛ x ⅞ inches (2.8 x 2.2 cm) long by ⅞ inch (2.2 cm) deep. Depending on the width and length of the glass pieces you cut, the overall size may change.

STEP BY STEP

1. Cut four pieces of glass sheet to make the sides of the bead. (If you don't know how to cut glass, contact your local stained glass supplies shop for assistance. You should be able to buy the glass you want and have them cut it to size for a fee.) Create some flat narrow strips of textured dry metal clay for a narrow trim on the bead.

2. Use decorative (or regular) scissors to cut a strip of metal clay paper three times the thickness of your glass sheet. Lightly wet each glass edge and wrap it with metal clay paper, overlapping the corners and working your way around the glass to frame it. Don't overdo the amount of water used or the metal clay paper will become mushy. Let the metal clay dry in position.

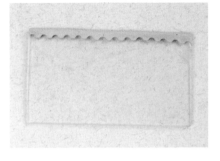

3. Using thick slip, stand the glass slides on their short ends and connect all four into a box formation by overlapping at the corners. Let the box dry in place. Caulk the seams and the corners for strength and appearance.

4. Clean up the seam areas. For the end caps, you can use a flat, two-card-thick sheet of plain dry metal clay that's decorated with syringe metal clay, or use a textured sheet.

5. Apply the end caps using a butt seam. (You can't miter the metal clay paper.) Use thick slip to attach the end caps, and allow them to dry.

6. Groom the seams, and drill and clean the holes. Give the bead the eagle eye and fire on a kiln shelf. Finish as desired.

Note: The bead shown has thin strips of textured metal clay appliquéd to two opposite sides of the bead. The other two sides are decorated with a syringe.

PORCUPINE BEAD

Implanted and fired wires hold half-drilled pearls, resulting in a uniquely shaped bead. Using gem balls instead of pearls could add a splash of color. After honing your skills on this project, you can dream up other mold shapes to create beads with similar modular characteristics.

MATERIALS

Polymer clay
Metal clay
Slip
20-gauge round wire, fine, sterling, or Argentium, 6 inches (15.2 cm) long
18 half-drilled pearls or gemstone balls, 4 to 5 mm in diameter

TOOLS

Basic Tool Kit (page 12)
Large, coarse file
Fine-tip marker
Jewelers' saw frame and blade
Texture plate
#60 drill bit in pin vise
Chain-nose pliers
Wire nippers
Small tweezers
Two-part epoxy
Toothpick

STEP BY STEP

1. Using polymer clay, fashion a curved wedge shape that is 1½ inches (3.8 cm) long by ⅝ inch (1.6 cm) wide at the thickest part of the wedge, and ¼ inch (6 mm) wide at the thinnest part of the wedge. The widest outside curve should have a radius of ¼ inch (6 mm) that tapers

to the edge. The shape should be a portion of a circle with a 1⅝-inch (4.1 cm) diameter.

Multiple views of the polymer clay form

2. Model the polymer clay shape as symmetrically as possible and bake it according to the manufacturer's instructions. If necessary, use a coarse file to even out the shape.

3. Using the fine-tip marker, draw a line around the circumference of the shape. Saw the shape into two pieces. Label one side A and the other side B on the flat parts of the pieces.

4. Lightly oil the two curved portions of the polymer shapes. Roll out some textured metal clay to two cards thick. Precut the metal clay into three half-moon shapes a little larger than your mold. Completely cover the polymer clay form with the textured clay and trim any excess. Set this piece aside to dry, and repeat the process on the other mold.

5. Remove the dried clay forms from the molds. Sweep the edges of the clay on a sheet of emery paper, flush to the table. Don't remove more clay than is necessary. Repeat this step for the other side.

6. Place the two clay pieces together, edge-to-edge, and check the fit. File, if needed. Use thick slip to glue the sides together, and set aside to dry. Clean any slip that has oozed on the outside of the seam. Reach into the inner seam as best you can, and caulk with clay to strengthen the seam.

Creating the Pins

1. Find the center of the arc and mark with a fine-tip marker or pencil. Using a #60 drill bit, drill a hole ⅛ inch (3 mm) on each side of the center mark. Drill two more holes on each side of the first holes ¼ inch (6 mm) apart. Drill two more holes ¼ inch (6 mm) from the previous holes, for a total of six holes.

(continued on next page)

2. Use chain-nose pliers and wire nippers to fashion three U-shaped pieces of 20-gauge round wire. Each will be a custom fit for each pair of holes, measuring ¼ x ¼ x ¼ inch (6 x 6 x 6 mm). Fit the wires into the

holes from the inside of the metal clay forms, using a small pair of tweezers. The two prongs will stick out about ³⁄₁₆ to ⁵⁄₁₆ inch (5 to 7 mm).

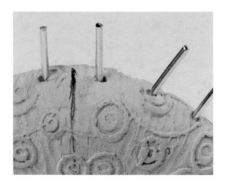

Trim down to size after firing to accommodate the pearls.

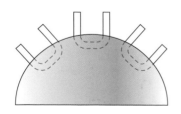

3. Secure the U-shaped pieces by applying slip to the inside on top of the wire. Let this dry. Repeat this process for the other two sets of holes until you have six protruding wires. Caulk with metal clay and fill in any gaps on the outside around the wires. Let this dry. Remove any excess clay from the seam areas.

4. Repeat the formation of the other two "lobes" of the bead in the same way. Use an emery board to file the three lobes flat on the open side. Check that the three half-moon shapes match in size.

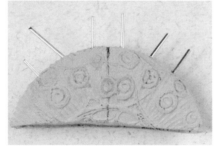

5. Create a very gentle concave curve on the flat edges by filing more material away on the inside of the flat, open side than on the points of the flat, open side. Bevel each textured edge at a shallow angle.

6. Use polymer clay as jigs to help in the construction and drying process. Attach two lobes to one another using thick slip and set up to dry in position. Each lobe will be positioned at 120° angles to the other lobes.

7. When dry, caulk the inside seam with metal clay for reinforcement. As you work, handle the piece with care—any undue pressure can break the seam. Attach the third lobe to the other two with a generous amount of slip, and set aside to dry. Groom the outside of the seams, caulking with clay as needed.

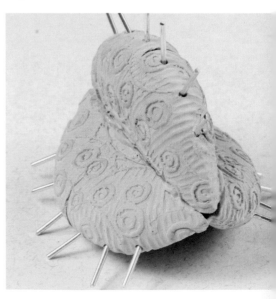

8. Carefully open some holes on the ends of the bead with a drill or a craft knife, to accommodate a chain or cord. Clean up any ragged edges. Fire the bead supported with vermiculite or a fiber blanket, and patina and finish as desired.

1. Fit a pearl or gemstone onto one of the protruding wires. Note how much wire needs to be nipped away, remove the pearl, and nip off only that amount of wire from the end. Refit the pearl to make sure you have removed enough wire. No wire should be visible when the pearl is sitting on its pin.

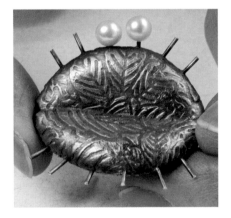

2. Mix up a small amount of epoxy. (You don't want to mix up all the epoxy you need, as it will set before you finish setting all the pearls.) Use a toothpick to coat the nipped wire with just enough glue, but not so much that it oozes out over the metal. Slip the pearl over the wire and twist as you lower it to eliminate air bubbles.

3. Repeat this process for the rest of the wires and pearls. Handle the bead carefully so as not to disturb previously set pearls. Set the bead aside and let the epoxy cure.

Variations

- Vary the number and size of the pearls or gemstone balls.
- Vary the number of lobes. This could be a four-lobed bead.
- Add kum boo or gold paste before finishing and setting the pearls.
- Use fully drilled pearls, gemstone balls, or glass beads, and make the wires long enough to secure the beads with a decorative spiral tip after threading them onto the wires.

COMPLEX CORE BEAD

Long spans of high-fire metal clay may need inner support, so I developed the core system described in this project to make really large hollow forms. A layer of paper clay does the job: The volcanic ash in it allows the paper clay to withstand the high temperatures of firing without shrinking or burning out, so it remains intact and rigid enough to support the metal clay until sintering is complete. Use this method for any type of hollow clay construction where sagging may be an issue. Be still my beating heart!

MATERIALS

Any moldable, combustible, core
material such as florist's foam
Old candles or paraffin
Paper clay
Metal clay
Slip

TOOLS

Basic Tool Kit (page 12)
Small saucepan to melt the wax
Large saucepan for the water bath
Stovetop or hot plate
Heat-proof gloves
Bamboo skewer
Paintbrush to apply hot wax
Tongs

Note: The complex core can be adapted to high-fire clay by making the outer wax layer 1/8 inch (3 mm) thick to accommodate the 30% shrinkage. For the lower firing clays that shrink only 12%, make the outer layer of wax 1/16 inch (2 mm) thick.

STEP BY STEP

1. Make your innermost core about 10% smaller than you would like your final form to be to make up for the additional layer of paper clay. Using the craft knife and florist's foam, cut out the basic shape for the innermost core, and mold it with your fingers.

Note: If you are using cork clay, wood clay, or any hard material for the core, you can skip the steps about adding wax.

2. Using the small and large saucepans to make a double boiler on the stovetop, melt the wax. Good ventilation is essential, so melt your wax using a vent fan in the kitchen, or on a hot plate outside. The aim is to melt the wax so that it is liquid, *not* so that it is boiling hot. Wax that is too hot is dangerous. Never leave the wax pot unattended during the waxing procedure. Wear heat-proof gloves while handling the pot and the hot wax.

3. Stick a bamboo skewer into your foam core where you'd like to place a bead hole. The skewer will also act as a handle. When the wax is ready,

paint a thin layer on the foam to stiffen the surface. Leave it to cool, and turn off the heat.

4. On a clean, lightly oiled work surface, roll out a three-card-thick sheet of *paper clay*, (**not** metal clay). Using a patchwork technique, cover the core completely, making sure the seams are well connected and smooth. Work around the skewer or take it out and reinsert it when you're finished covering the core. Let the paper clay dry and harden for 24 hours. It is essential that the paper clay layer be bone dry.

5. Wipe off your work area and tools of all paper clay so as to not contaminate your metal clay. Heat up the wax pot. When the wax is melted, paint or dip your core (using tongs) to build up a layer of wax. This wax layer provides a buffer space during the firing so that the metal clay can shrink to the paper clay layer without restriction. If you were to build the metal clay directly on the paper clay, the metal clay would have nowhere to go as it shrank, resulting in cracking and separation of the clay.

(continued on next page)

Try to build up the wax consistently. Check the depth by pushing a needle tool or straight pin gently into the wax until it hits the hard paper clay. This will tell you how much wax is layered. Poke the needle in a number of different areas to confirm consistent depth. Turn off the heat and let the core cool. Remove the skewer from the core.

6. Enlarge the hole and create a second bead hole by using a craft knife or drill bit, digging through the layer of wax and paper clay to the first core. I make these holes a bit larger than usual to aid in the removal of the paper clay after firing. Clean away any wax and paper clay bits so they don't get mixed into the metal clay.

7. Roll out the metal clay to two cards thick. Use a patchwork technique to piece the clay together, covering the core. Take care to create well-connected seams. Use slip to completely close each seam area.

8. For the appliquéd shapes, roll out a sheet of metal clay to three cards thick. Begin by outlining the bead holes with circles. Attach each appliqué shape with slip. Gently press with your fingertips to make sure the appliqué conforms to the contour of the basic form.

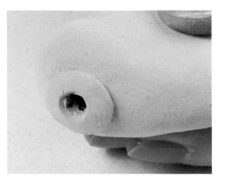

9. While the appliqué shape is still soft, use the cone-shaped clay tool to poke decorative depressions around the perimeter of the shape, to mimic rivets. Cover the surface of the bead with random shapes in the same manner. Leave it to dry, and then fire the bead supported with vermiculite or a fiber blanket. Before you remove the paper clay, do any additional firing as needed. Finish as desired.

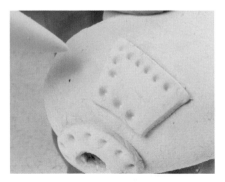

10. Using a needle tool, chip the paper clay away through the bead holes. The paper clay should break apart easily and fall out of the holes when you shake the bead.

MARGARITE PARKER GUGGOLZ
Restless, 2007
Pendant, 0.5 x 3.5 x 9 cm
Fine silver, 22-karat gold, sterling silver,
liver of sulfur; formed, fired, strung,
fabricated, patinated
PHOTO BY RALPH GABRINER

TOP RIGHT

NANCY KARPEL
Seaform Beads, 1998
4.5 x 3 x .7 cm
Left, fine silver PMC, enamel;
center, fine silver PMC, sapphire;
right, fine silver PMC, enamel
PHOTO BY FRANK POOLE

RIGHT

CLAIRE HOLLIDAY
November, 2007
4.2 x 3.2 x 3.2 cm
Fine silver; patinated
PHOTO BY DEAN POWELL

METAL CLAY AND
LAMPWORKED
GLASS BEAD

This bead combines my dual passions for metal clay and glass, and it requires basic lampworking skills. I make the core of the bead from metal clay, which is fired and then tumbled to a high mirror finish that shines through the glass applied over it.

MATERIALS

Metal clay
Syringe metal clay
Slip
Copper wire, 8 gauge,
    or large-diameter cord
Soda Lime glass rod
    in any light, transparent color*

TOOLS

Basic Tool Kit (page 12)
Texture plate of your choice
Tumbler, shot, and burnishing
    compound
Lampworking tools and supplies
Brass brush or liver of sulfur
    (optional)

*Hard glass or borosilicate glass is not recommended because the temperatures necessary to melt these glasses are dangerously close to the melting point of fine silver.

STEP BY STEP

1. Lightly oil a drinking straw. Prepare a two-card-thick textured metal clay sheet. Or make a tube from plain sheet and decorate it later.

2. Cut a rectangle that's ⅝ x 1 inch (1.6 x 2.5 cm) long. Lay the short side of the rectangle on the straw and wrap it around the straw. Cut through both layers with a craft knife to create a perfectly fitting seam, and attach the seam with slip.

3. Once it has dried, groom the outside of the seam by flicking off any excess slip, and caulking any gaps with clay. At this point, if you are making a hollow glass bead, you can use your syringe to create a low relief texture on the cylinder.

4. Gently slip the cylinder off the straw and strengthen the inside of the seam with clay. Allow the seam to dry, and then use an emery board to file the ends of the cylinder to a 90° angle.

Creating the End Caps

1. Roll out some metal clay to two cards thick. If you like, it can be textured clay. Cut out two circles that are ½ inch (1.3 cm) in diameter, and set aside to dry. Circles are best for the shape of the end caps, but if your lampworking skills allow, you can experiment with different shapes such as squares.

2. File the edges of the circles so that they are smooth and consistent. Find the center of each circle and use a drill or the end of a craft knife to create a hole the same size as the inner diameter of the cylinder.

3. Secure each circle end cap to the cylinder with slip. Groom the seams by cleaning any excess slip and caulking with clay where necessary. Use the syringe to add decorative elements to the end caps. Check to see that the syringe decoration is securely attached to the surface of the circle. Let the piece dry, and then fire it supported with vermiculite or a fiber blanket.

4. Thread a copper wire or large-diameter cord through the cylinder and twist or bend the ends to prevent the stainless steel shot from lodging itself in the opening of the spool. Place it in a tumbler with shot and burnishing liquid for about 3 hours, or until you achieve a high mirror finish.

5. Dip a mandrel in bead release and thread the spool onto the mandrel. Dry it horizontally, and then clean off any bead release that may have gotten into the inside of the spool shaft. The bead release on the outside of the end caps can be easily cleaned off after annealing.

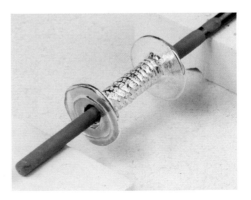

(continued on next page)

6. To make a hollow bead on your spool, begin gathering the glass in the crevice between the end cap and the shaft. Start a gather on the other side and continue piling on the glass until the two sides meet and there are no air holes. Heat the glass until it "puffs" out and smoothes.

7. If you like, you can add dots to the surface, but don't add too many elements or you won't be able to see the decorated metal clay shaft through the glass. Anneal as usual, and remove the bead from the mandrel. Clean off the bead release from the inside of the hole.

8. This bead can be tumbled, but remember to thread wire through the hole. Alternately, a brass brush can be used to finish the end caps. The tumbler, a brass brush, or patina chemicals will not harm the glass.

9. If using liver of sulfur, place the bead in a warm solution and bring the temperature up. Dropping a glass bead into simmering liquid will probably result in cracking. Also, don't rinse the piece in cold water to stop the action of the chemical or you might crack the glass. Use a very warm water rinse instead, and allow the bead to air cool.

CINDY PANKOPF
Fool's Cage Beads, 2007
Largest, 36 x 23 x 23 mm;
smallest, 15 x 23 x 23 mm
Silver metal clay, Moretti glass;
lampworked
PHOTO BY ARTIST

Variations

- Try making the glass a solid bead instead of a hollow one.
- Lengthen the spool for a bigger bead, depending on your lampworking skills.

BARBARA BECKER SIMON
Tautology, 2006
1.5 x 50 cm
Glass beads, fine-silver spool;
lampworked
PHOTO BY ROBERT DIAMANTE

BARBARA BECKER SIMON
Green Glass/PMC bead, 2006
2.5 x 2.3 cm
Glass, fine-silver spool;
lampworked
PHOTO BY ROBERT DIAMANTE

ACKNOWLEDGMENTS

I can't remember when I wasn't making things. My mother, a graduate of Pratt Institute in advertising design, and my mechanical engineer father (a Pratt alumnus, too), contributed genes, encouragement, and love throughout their lives. This is my fundamental and most important acknowledgment.

I've had the impact of unforgettable teachers at all levels of my education: Mr. Lyons in high school, Professors Stein and Matzdorf in college, and Fred Fenster and J. Fred Woell in graduate school. Without their knowledge and guidance, I would not be the artist or—just as important—the teacher I have become. J. Fred Woell shared with me his simple but brilliant methods for constructing the Wire Armature Bead, the Sheet Metal Armature Bead, and the Pebble Bead in this book.

I humbly thank all the students who allowed me to pass on the things I've learned. You've contributed to my education more than you can imagine.

I'm so grateful to all my friends and acquaintances in the world of metal clay. I've benefited immensely from the constant free flow of ideas and inspiration. I need to name names: Tim McCreight, my friend and mentor who "discovered" me tinkering away in Florida; CeCe Wire, Chris Darway, and Celie Fago, my fellow "pioneers"; and my gifted friends Terry Kovalcik, Tonya Davidson, and Jeanette Landenwitch. Thanks, each of you, for the priceless information and all the jolly hours.

"Arigatou gozaimasu" to the clever folks in Japan who developed the first metal clay. What would we be missing if Dr. Morikawa hadn't had his brainstorm?!

I must acknowledge my friends at Rio Grande who have been so enormously supportive of our efforts to spread the "metal clay news." My progress with this wonderful material wouldn't have been nearly as swift without their help. Thank you Alan Bell, Kevin Whitmore, Gail Philippi, Virginia Dickson, and Yvonne Padilla.

Thanks to the folks at Lark who helped make this book possible. Marthe Le Van guided me through developing its manuscript; Nathalie Mornu and Kathleen McCafferty edited it; Dana Irwin styled a gorgeous book; editorial assistant Dawn Dillingham managed the gallery; and intern Jacob Biba lent a helping hand.

Robin Gregory and Thom Gaines kept all aspects of art production running smoothly.

I'm grateful for the talents of Rob Stegmann and Stewart O'Shields, the photographers who made my work shine under the bright lights. A thankful nod to ARCH who so generously provided the clay earth plaster backgrounds for our project photography (ARCH: Architectural Accents and Gallery, Asheville, NC: www.thearchnc.com).

I'm also compelled to acknowledge Max Minor, Syrinja Kurasawa, Jessica Braun, Hansie Montoya, Isabelle Bubacco, John Bobby Rockhill, Singha Jones, Chet Bolins, Crakky O'Vilet, Dusty Rhodes, and, most especially, Babbette Belmondo for their contributions to the well-being of my psyche.

Finally, I would end where I began, with thanks to my family, near and far, here and gone; Sylvie, my own personal cheering section; and Michael, who, through thick and thin, has been steadfast in his support of the stubborn artist he married.

ABOUT THE
AUTHOR

Photo by James Borcherdt

Barbara Becker Simon earned a B.S. in Art Education at the State University of New York at New Paltz, and received an M.F.A. in Metalwork and Jewelry from the University of Wisconsin-Madison. She has been a goldsmith for more than 40 years, and has taught at the University of Wisconsin-Stout in Menomonie, Wisconsin; Iowa State University; Edison Community College in Fort Myers, Florida; the Penland School of Crafts; and the Arrowmont School of Arts and Crafts.

Barbara crisscrosses the United States as a Senior Instructor for the Rio Rewards Precious Metal Clay Certification Program, and has taught in Japan—the birthplace of metal clay—and more recently in Australia, where she also taught beadmaking.

In addition to her metalwork, Barbara has gained international attention for her lampworked glass beads and jewelry. Her signature hollow core vessels are featured on the covers of several books on lampworking, and included in *1000 Glass Beads* (Lark, 2004). Barbara's glass beads are in the collection of the Bead Museum in Washington, DC; The Bead Museum in Glendale, Arizona; and the Kobe Lampwork Glass Museum in Kobe, Japan.

In 2007, Barbara won second-place for her metal clay in the prestigious Saul Bell Design Award Competition. Barbara's glass, metalwork, and writing has appeared in *Lapidary Journal*, and her work is featured in a number of books, including *Creative Metal Clay Jewelry: Techniques, Projects, Inspiration* (Lark, 2003), and *New Directions in Metal Clay* (Lark, 2007), both by CeCe Wire.

OPPOSITE PAGE
BARBARA BECKER SIMON
Maltese Fish, 2000
Focal bead, 4.5 x 5 x 2 cm
Fine silver, synthetic sapphire, freshwater pearls, glass, sterling silver; hollow bead created on complex core
PHOTO BY LARRY SANDERS

INDEX

CATHERINE WITHERELL
Handful of Beads, 2007
Largest, 5 x 4 x 1 cm
Metal clay, sterling silver wire, syringe; hand fabricated
PHOTO BY ARTIST

CONTRIBUTING
ARTISTS